Confessions of a Neglected African Daughter

*To Gordon
with Best wishes

Kwasi
12/15/15*

Kwasi Bosompem

Confessions of a Neglected African Daughter

Acknowledgments

To Dedeli for her hard work to support young women around the world

Library of Congress
Cataloging in Publication Data
ISBN 0-9649351-0-4 : $15.00

Published by
TPI
4415 Eagle Ct.
Waldorf, MD. 20603
e-mail: somb22@aol.com

Printed in the United States of America

October 2015
King Printing Company
www.kingprinting.com

Dedicated to Rodney and Daphne

CHAPTER 1
Home Sweet Home, Not!

Beyond the banks of River Birim in the eastern woodlands of Ghana lies the town of Akim Oda, the traditional and administrative seat of the Kotoku people. The terrain of Akim Oda is undulating, and the tropical forests are full of fruits and food products. The land has been cultivated over the years; however, the soil is still as fertile as ever. Semi-commercial agricultural production and food from the sprawling farms support the population. Other natural resources such as timber, minerals, and the produce from the rich forests are the economic base. The basic occupations of the people in the area are mining and farming. Diamonds and gold are also plentiful in the vast Akim territory. The precious diamonds of the world are dredged along the banks of the river while foreign companies mine the gold. Farmers in the area have been digging and tilling the land for years. The boarding school at nearby Akim Awisa has produced professionals, including doctors, lawyers, and teachers. As such, the town has flourished all these years.

Since most of these professionals work outside the town and in foreign countries, their constant remittances home, as well as trips and vacations to the homeland, served to motivate most of the youth, including a teenager by the name of Akosua Sojourner Mensah. Being in the local high school, Akosua was determined to have a future and be like the number of professionals who often returned home. That was her ambition. As every weekend passed, the local bus station became the main hub and activity center as families celebrated their children's homecomings or bid farewell to their sons and daughters returning to their homes and places of employment. The local restaurant and bar at the major bus terminal was always busy. Families, relatives, friends, and lovers gathered to listen to brass band music while awaiting the arrival or departure of loved ones.

Akim Oda itself, being cosmopolitan in population, was composed of an old town separated by a railway line from the

1

commercially and residentially mixed new town. Tribes and clans lived in a mixed area separated from commercial and business activities. It was a sprawling African town.

Mr. John Mensah, the head of the Mensah household, had five wives. They served him as if he was a king in the town. Mrs. Joanne Mensah was Akosua's mother. However, the probability that Mr. Mensah would have an affair or marry a new-found love during a business trip was always very high. They all lived in the large compound house attached to a three-story mansion.

The compound house was about 60 feet by 50 feet in area. Each wife lived in a condominium unit that had a separate bath. There were five kitchens and two other main baths and toilets for the rest of the household. The old man himself lived on the third floor of the mansion. The young women and the boys without their mothers and other illegitimate children lived on the second and the third floors respectively.

Today, Polygamy in Ghana is considered an old and anachronistic social behavior. It was very common in the towns in the 1960's and 1970's but now prevails only in the villages and the more remote settlements. During these times, Mr. Mensah had not stopped his love pursuits and polygamous life. It was not possible to count all the children in the house. Noise was terrible at home when all the children gathered in the evenings. The total household on such noisy evenings included neighbors and friends, and at times the number of people could not be estimated. Sometimes, Akosua could not exactly remember the total household, especially the young women. There was always a different face in the house, and she never knew who Mr. Mensah's latest fiancée was or who her half-sisters whom she had never met were. Despite his large family in those years, Mr. Mensah was still having babies.

In Mr. Mensah's household, the old order never changed. Early in the morning, everyone in the household had his or her duties. Some fetched water from either the public taps or River Birim. Others swept the whole compound while the strong lads vacuumed the rooms, floors, tables, and other furniture in the living room.

2

It was trouble for a child in the household to refuse to do his or her duties. That person would receive punishment from Mr. Mensah. Roll call was regular, and inspection of work was strict. Meals were also a problem at times for the illegitimate boys around. Those who had their mothers around were always assured of a full three square meals a day. The illegitimate boys, especially, suffered the most. They had to be around to be attentive to the bell of Mr. Mensah signaling he had finished eating. The person closest to the dining room then had to run to collect the leftovers and carry the food to the ground floor where all the boys would eat the food from the same bowl. At times, you could count about 10 hands in a plate. They all ate with their fingers from the same dish. Some boys were always around as they could not afford to be late, let alone be absent.

Mr. Mensah had meant to keep a very strict discipline and forced lifestyle on Akosua and had sworn to make her an example in everything. When she was 18, her father forbade Akosua from entertaining friends, let alone having a boyfriend. He prevented all his daughters from dating men or even playing outside the home. Most evenings he relaxed in his gold decorated special chair and enjoyed the evening's blowing breeze. He always had his favorite drink mixed with herbs placed under his chair. He usually took sips and left the bottle under the chair. One such evening, he looked around the compound and shouted, "Akosua! Akosua!"

"Yes, Papa?" Akosua replied.

"All right, Akosua. I just called to ensure you were home," he answered.

Akosua was one of the most beautiful girls in Mr. Mensah's household. She had a dark complexion and was about five feet two inches tall. She was very intelligent; however, the conditions at home were not conducive for her. Mr. Mensah called her every minute. At times, he just called for no other reason but to make sure Akosua had not gone out. At other times, there was the usual work to be done at home. He was not interested in the education of his children. As the society allowed, he shirked a major social responsibility as a father. It was also common knowledge that Mr. Mensah would never allow his children to attend a university or

3

college. After one's basic high school education, even a career or training school was a hard sell. He would have preferred that everyone become a businessperson. Anything with immediate return on investments was more meaningful to him. His ideas and thoughts about college made it impossible to discuss any educational plans with him. Truly, Akosua did not remember a day she ever had a serious conversation on her educational plans with her father. It was difficult because the man was always angry with someone or something. Mr. Mensah used to be a strong man who had worked hard for his wealth; however, he was getting older and poorer.

One evening in the hot summer months, as Mr. Mensah relaxed on his gold decorated chair on the porch of his three-story mansion, he called Akosua again.

"Akosua, Akosua!" shouted Mr. Mensah.

"Papa?" Akosua replied.

"Bring me a toothpick and a paper towel immediately. Hurry!" he ordered and continued, "I warn you again, Akosua especially, and all of you in this house, these days it is not safe to be out very late in the night because of the traditional celebrations in the town. I warn all of you, my daughters, not to stay out late at night. If anyone entertains a boyfriend and becomes pregnant before marriage, that person will be out of my household. Teenage pregnancy is what I hate most," he concluded. "Thank you," he said to Akosua as she brought the toothpick and the paper towel.

Akosua tried to study every evening for her High School Diploma Examinations, and she worried a lot about her future. She was not happy at home. It was really affecting her studies. She realized that attending school was not fun anymore.

The old students told her that they had seen a better life in the year's gone bye, and Akosua could also see several signs that the past had been better. Today, there were no more subsidized lunches with bananas, rice, and fried plantain at noon. She did much manual labor always. Imagine a teenager like Akosua Mensah cutting the grass on the lawn with a cutlass. In this modern age of technology, she could not believe doing this. She realized it had been years since Ghana got independence and the British

4

packed up, and left the land of gold. In these modern times, Akim-Oda High School could not even afford a mower to cut the grass. As such, students did manual labor all the time. She thought it would destroy her natural black beauty if she continued to work like that every day.

At school, some of her teachers were always absent, and she did not have a permanent teacher. Within that year alone, five different teachers had come and left the school. Her school compound was not as it had been. All the date palm trees and flowers were dead. The remaining lawns and gardens were in a poor state, as if they had never been maintained. Most of the flowers on the school campus had been destroyed.

Sanitation and basic infrastructure were major problems. The once beautiful natural landscape was no longer beautiful. Even the old church building was in ruins although the church community was as organized as ever. Money was hard to come by to rehabilitate the building. In effect, this problem was making church attendance very difficult for some Christians in the town. The church building could have collapsed any time. The walls were cracked, and the ceilings leaked. Water dripped from the ceiling during prayer sessions. Efforts of the once-good Christians and others were being hampered.

On the local economy, producer prices of raw materials had fallen low. They were worth nothing. Producer prices could not cope with inflationary trends. The over dependence on one commercial crop without any diversification was a major problem. When the local economy failed to sustain itself, the farmer was disregarded in society. Mr. John Mensah could not be working for such low returns in such subsistence farming. That was why he had turned a jack-of-all-trades, transacting business, farming, buying and selling general merchandise, and engaging in stone contracting. Even he had lost money on most of these businesses.

Akosua never understood whether these economic hardships were the main reason for the actions of Mr. Mensah toward her. She really never understood why her father was making life uncomfortable for her in the large household. Akosua was not happy at home at all. There was much pressure on her from her parents that she did not understand. She began to suspect the reason when her mother started discussing marriage affairs with her. Her mother was fond of talking about a happy family life and all the nice things about getting married after school. Akosua realized her parents were arranging a marriage for her to a rich old farmer by the name of Papa James immediately after high school.

"Oh, Akosua," said her mother one evening, "you have to plan your future. At 18 years, you are a young woman now. Some of your other friends have their marriages planned at your age. They will marry the most respectable man they can find and settle down as homemakers while planning the birth of their babies. Some of your friends are even doing well in home business and raising their children. You have to plan your life and think of what to do after your examinations. We will help you find a respectable man to marry."

This annoyed Akosua, and she protested vehemently.

"Why me! Why me! Please do not arrange any marriage for me. I will plan my marriage when I am ready. In these modern times, young women of my age group do not believe in the old society and the arranged marriages. You have made my life very difficult. You have separated me from others in town. You have blocked a thousand and one opportunities. And now, you are telling me what to do," Akosua screamed. She could not believe what her mother had told her. She ran to her room and slammed the door behind her.

Mr. Mensah immediately walked in and shouted, "What is happening? Akosua! Be careful! Akosua! Do not say that. It is not respectful to speak to your mother like that. You are a disrespectful, lazy, young person."

Her father scolded her more that evening. "This will be the first and last time you confront your mother in such harsh words," Mr. Mensah said. "I can easily kick you out of the house after all." Mrs. Mensah also did not stop scolding and warning her.

Akosua remained indoors most of the time after this confrontation with her parents. She thought of several options of what to do with her life after school. She could not plan anything without peace of mind, as well as moral and financial support.

6

"What sort of parents are these?" she said to herself. "They do not want to make life comfortable for me. It has been so difficult to study for my examinations and continue my education as others do. There is always trouble in the house day after day. I have to do something before it's too late.".

Some minutes later, Mr. Mensah shouted again. "Akosua! Akosua!"

She did not respond this time, but thought to herself "I might as well face this old man. I have a month before my final examinations, and I bet I'll never have peace of mind."

"Akosua," continued Mr. Mensah. He asked one of the girls in the house to call Akosua from her room. It was definitely another insult on Akosua, although she did not know the reason for the call. However, she stood up and walked toward her father. The old man was very annoyed.

Seeing her, he burst out, "You! Akosua, I warned and advised you to keep away from that student. I hear that you jump walls in the night and follow this boy."

Mr. Mensah was angry, but he was saying the truth. He was as furious as ever and wanted to flog Akosua with his big cane as she walked toward him. Immediately, Akosua knelt down and burst into tears. Mr. Mensah complained that he had heard many stories about Akosua and the boy in the neighborhood.

Mr. Mensah did not realize that Akosua had grown and matured. He shouted and scolded Akosua all the time. It was difficult for her to explain the story to him since he was just not interested in any explanation.

Akosua was a young woman and could take care of herself. The idea of an arranged marriage was unheard of in any major and modern town in Ghana. However, Mr. Mensah and his old-age friends were stuck in it and did not want to change.

Akosua was unimpressed with her father's actions but rather crazy about Essien, the boy her parents and Papa James disliked. Essein was her high school sweetheart and they had been going out for almost a year without Mr. Mensah's knowledge. The two were very close friends. However Mr. Mensah had been hearing reports from the neighbors, and especially from Papa James who wanted Akosua for marriage.

One Tuesday evening before the strict warning by Mr. Mensah, Akosua and Essien had gone to a concert. That day, a concert group, the Star-Jokers, had come to the Premier Hotel at Akim Oda. Everyone was out in the night. Essien whistled the special greeting they used for each other and called for Akosua. Hearing the whistle, Akosua stole a duplicate key and sneaked out of the house to the concert with Essien. Mr. Mensah did not notice.

Akosua enjoyed herself that night. People from all walks of life in the town came to the dance. The music was loud and the place was rocking. Akosua could not resist such an event. After all, her classmates who were also preparing for the High School Diploma Examinations were all present at the concert.

Essien had often been requesting Akosua to go to bed with him. No matter how many promises and requests she made to him to wait until after her final examinations, he would not listen. Akosua loved Essien but did not really believe in teenage premarital sex. That night after the Star Jokers' concert, Essien tried to make love to Akosua. She resisted him during a struggle.

It all happened near the football grounds on the route to her home. The two were walking when they saw someone with a flashlight on the street. Essien pushed Akosua down onto the lawn and said quietly, "Get down! It may be your father carrying the flashlight. He must be returning home. He must have spent the night in the house of the owner of the restaurant across the road."

Essien gave Akosua a good kiss. Essien realized he was up to a tough fight, so he held her very tight with all his strength. Akosua pushed Essien off and stood up while Essien laid down, tired but still pleading to kiss her again. It was a quiet, late night and the wind was blowing. There were still noises on the streets after the concert. Akosua then talked to Essien, promising him all the best of love if he could only wait until after her final examinations.

As Essien still lay down, Akosua left him and went straight home. She knew if it was Mr. Mensah who passed by with the flashlight then he might be looking for her.

Mr. Mensah was, however, at home still awake. He was looking down the street waiting for any of his children who went out in the night to come by. Akosua saw him from afar and hurriedly entered the house through the back door. Akosua knew about safe sex and abstinence education and the whole sex purity stuff. Although, she had not been taught in school, she had read and heard a lot from her friends about AIDS and many other sexully transmitted diseases, or STDs. Akosua wanted to be different from the other girls and all the marital problems in her household. She wanted to make a statement and believed in at least completing her higher education before getting involved with any man.

It was even a taboo to discuss sex in public during those times. All she knew were stories by her classmates and other friends. She even found it difficult to believe some of them. The stories and gossip about love and relationships were a way to keep them entertained at school. Even so, Akosua felt ashamed to talk to her friends at school about what Essien tried to do to her after the concert. They had warned her previously about the possibilities of Essien forcing her to have sex. She did not worry much that night because it was the second time Essien had attempted to do that. In her mind she was more worried about all the problems at home than about Essien.

Akosua remembered the concert the night before. That night the Star Jokers did their most popular song, called "Show Your Love." It was Akosua's favorite. She had memorized all the words. She was totally thrilled by the song. Days after the concert she was still singing the tune. It went like this.

"Show your love
Sister your love
If you show your love
I will show mine too"

Akosua did not know exactly who might have told Mr. Mensah about her night with Essien. But still, he had found out. The days after the concert were unbearable for Akosua. In some ways, it was not that different from other normal days, except there was a closer watch on her. But Mr. Mensah kept shouting and

9

complaining about Essien. This was an attempt to stop Akosua from going out with him. Any time she attempted to study, there would be a call from her parents. There was also the same routine in the house as always. Either the toilet must be cleaned, dishes washed, or laundry done. There was always work in the household for Akosua. To her parents, this was an effort to train her as a good homemaker and prepare her for marriage. Neither of these ideas pleased Akosua because she was not happy and was scared by the thought of an arranged marriage.

Her half-sisters and their friends had been paying more particular attention to their night studies, which they found very interesting. Supervision was a little bit relaxed. Akosua therefore asked permission from her parents to attend night studies which were then very popular in some of the local high schools in Ghana. Each day from 7:00 to 10:00 in the evening, students would go to their schools for night studies to do their homework and more than just the homework. Various classes used the time for brainstorming on problem topics, group discussions, and play.

There was one big electric lamp in Akosua's class. It was on top of a cupboard in the right corner of the classroom. There were also smaller lamps on the desks. These were used as backup in case of power failure. During intermittent short breaks from night studies, the students gathered on the porch of the school building and played cat and mouse games. Others just gossiped as an effort to release tension. They all studied and had fun during these hours. There were several places on the school compound, where they gathered in groups. Usually they were near the bathhouse or in front of the principal's office. The same old happiness always prevailed at night studies. Young people had fun between studies. Some students bought fried ripe plantain from the streets and ate in the corridors. Others who brought food from home gathered at other suitable places.

Akosua was not motivated to study seriously at home, but rather went to night studies each time. It was natural to meet with her friends at school because they were all preparing for the examinations. With her colleagues around, she always had some good students available to help her in mathematics and other

subjects. As the pending high school diploma examinations drew closer, she requested fewer household duties. Surprisingly, her parents agreed and were less harsh on her. She had all the time to study and did what she wanted to do at school. Since there were no formal classes, the students held private studies in chemistry, biology, and mathematics, in which some of the young women had problems. Akosua had other student partners to help her in physics and other science subjects during the night studies. Generally, the females were considered as doing well in subjects such as Geography, English, and History, and they also enjoyed arts and crafts, cookery, sewing, and other activities. This was reinforcing the old adage in the society that the sciences were very hard and not meant for females; these were subjects for the men. Of course, it was not true and was disproved in later years when more females graduated with honors in the sciences from many colleges.

One afternoon, Akosua was relaxing at home when her girlfriend Grace called her. Grace was the same age as Akosua. She was lighter in complexion. She had some news.

"Akosua, there is a new guy in town who does tutoring to get students ready for their diploma exams. This is a great chance for us. I know him personally and we should see this man. Let's do it," she suggested.

The man was called Mr. Williams, and he was a professional tutor on the Fourth Street North in Akim Oda. After Grace mentioned this, Akosua readily followed because she knew Grace loved her and wanted her to pass the examination. They took a taxi straight to Mr. Williams' office.

"There he stands," Grace pointed to Mr. Williams.

He was a man in his fifties. Mr. Williams welcomed and briefed them on the various items on the program before their registration. The tutorials available were only for the English examination. After a while, Grace followed him to the conference room. Akosua stayed behind. She was alone for about 20 minutes. Akosua felt sleepy and wanted to leave. Soon, Grace and Mr. Williams came back into the room and Mr. Williams asked Akosua some questions on her past English examinations. The two then listened while Mr. Williams showed them the success stories of his program and testimonials from past students. He gave them a sample English essay topic and guidelines to practice at home. Time was running fast for Akosua, so she signaled to Grace that they should be leaving. As they left the premises, Mr. Williams whispered to Akosua. Akosua and Grace thought the man was handsome, and both admired him. Neither of them complained nor made any negative comment about him.

At home, Akosua copied the essay guide and format from Grace. They later agreed to pay him another visit after the examinations. Since it was days before the examinations, Akosua felt she had no choice but to inform her half-sisters and other friends of the new English format preparation guide. She told them that Mr. Williams had asked them to prepare a paper on the happiest day in their lives. Everyone thought they had received a sure tip on what the exam content would be.

This topic as an English paper was very easy for Akosua. She did her research, wrote it and had it corrected by other teachers who were good in English and essay writing. Soon the news had spread among all candidates in the school and other schools that there was a sure tip on the English paper. Now that they thought they knew the topic, it was a simple matter of writing the story clearly with the appropriate English sentences.

Akosua knew that the examiners would be looking for sentence construction, spelling, and use of phrases, vocabulary, and organization. Writing about the happiest and most interesting day in her life stirred up Akosua's most treasured memories and thoughts. The happiest day in Akosua's life could have been one of several. She could have considered the day when the Star Jokers came to town. That had been a very happy and memorable day for her. Essien gave her a wonderful treat, although he had made unwanted advances. Akosua could remember another happy day in her life, when it rained all day. That was a weekend that she had no studies. She did not join the family on a trip to the farm. She went with Essien and they visited the local park that whole day. Essien had taken Akosua to lunch that day because it was her birthday. She could have prepared very well on all these scenes, and could have written perfectly on any of them. However, she felt they were not very interesting topics for the school examinations.

On a second thought, she chose a particular day when the old man celebrated a family reunion at home. That day her mother gave her newly designed family reunion clothes. The menu was of turkey soup and rice and there was much to eat. Akim Oda Brass Band No. 2 provided music. On that day, the old man invited his friends. Grace came too, since she was a close family friend. Mr. Mensah did the customary rites with the slaughter of a sheep. After that, a local choir group performed. The family reunion was full of fun and each person had a wonderful time.

That particular reunion was one of a kind. The research on Akosua's family history was made known, and a family tree was prepared on a sheet of drawing paper. This was read out loud and also distributed to all members. Special prayers were said for the departed ones. The family used the occasion to get to know each other. They were so many that it was very difficult to remember names.

Akosua prepared this chosen topic very well. She placed emphasis on the importance of the family reunion, which her father celebrated every year. The family reunion celebrations were a chronicle of important family events and that was the reason why she chose it as her essay topic

It was not surprising that Akosua was very nervous about the pending high school diploma examinations. The exams were on a Friday, a popular and a noted event day in the town. It was a great day for every parent with school children. Grace called Akosua early that morning. With their pens, soft pencils, erasers, and rulers, they set off to the examination center. There were more smart school boys and girls that morning than ever before. Essien called to Akosua and wished her good luck.

The big school bell rang five times, and they all entered the examination hall. The first paper was on geography. It was followed by math, biology, and a general paper. Since Akosua did not trust herself in the general paper, she was very careful. There were five-minute breaks between the papers, and then came the

English essay. Each candidate had very high expectations for this paper. Each had decided to write well, as planned.

The supervisor called the candidates to order, and then held the large envelope containing the questions. He raised his voice and said, "I open these papers in the name of the Almighty."

He took the question papers out and distributed them face down on each desk and then ordered, "Don't look or turn your papers over until you are told to do so." He repeated this twice. From the last row, he walked up to the front of the class and glanced at his watch.

"Turn over, read, and start work," he shouted.

Akosua was still nervous. She tried to catch a glimpse of the other candidates, hoping to see smiling faces. She was very hesitant to read the question paper. Finally when she read the paper, it was very different. Wow! The English essay was difficult. What a surprise! It was a clear shock. The essay topic was:*"A Job Description of the work of an Auditing firm showing problems faced by auditors in their profession in the modern world"*

"The examiners have tricked us," Akosua thought.

Other candidates had surprised looks on their faces. Yes, it was all over their faces! They could not blame their teachers, nor Mr. Williams with his so-called tutorial and preparation guides. The topic was just an unexpected one. None of the tutorial guide topics and questions even came up. Some of the candidates had no idea about auditing.

The supervisor was strict. He took strides through the rows of desks and tables, so they could not talk among themselves as they had wanted to. Sixty minutes passed away. Another 30 minutes passed. Akosua expected the supervisor to have stopped them by now. Finally he shouted, "Get ready to stop work."

A few minutes later he raised his voice and shouted, "Stop Work!"

The class was quiet. Many students were happy about the whole examination except for the English essay. Others, like Akosua, were more shocked and surprised. She thought the paper was just okay although she had very little knowledge about auditing and could not resist the shock. Some of the students found it hard even to settle down to write anything meaningful. After the examinations were over, Akosua worried about getting a good grade on the English paper.

Later, some of her classmates called to share their thoughts on the English paper. Grace also called and suggested that they visit Mr. Williams to make a report. They agreed that Akosua would have lunch with Essien first, and then meet Grace later. Akosua had planned not to go home immediately. She knew she would finish the examinations at midday that Friday, but she had informed her household that the examinations would be over in the evening. She could then use the afternoon hours to celebrate in her own way. The fact that she had completed her high school education marked an important milestone in her life. It brought several thoughts to her about what she was going to do after school. All that advice from her mother about business and the expectations of an arranged marriage to an old, rich farmer was like a nightmare to her.

Her day was planned as she wanted, and she did her best to be on time. She hurried to see Essien, hoping to meet Grace later. Essien was already home waiting in his backyard garden. Akosua never used the main entrance to visit Essien. She was always afraid that someone would report her to Mr. Mensah. Essien signaled her to pass through the rear gate entrance. He gave her soda and some biscuits. Essien could understand her feelings about the examinations and did not want to discuss anything on the English paper. After a brief moment, he brought Akosua some light green soup and rice. Later, Akosua requested to leave. She said goodbye to Essien, although he thought she would have stayed much longer. Her plan was to meet Grace and follow up with Mr. Williams. Essien reluctantly understood her when she requested to leave.

Akosua took a shortcut to their rendezvous. Grace was already waiting. She spoke quietly to Akosua. "You look smart and full of pleasures, dear," Grace said.

"Essien was simple and understanding," Akosua replied.

The two then turned toward the office of Mr. Williams at the northern end of town. They got there in a short time and found Mr. Williams waiting. They were offered soft drinks, but they refused. Mr. Williams spoke first in a quiet mood saying, "I heard your examinations were difficult."

"We were surprised how the examiners could have presented these papers. It surprised everyone," Grace replied. "Everyone has been complaining, and the bad news around the town was on the English essay."

"I'm sure you are all worried," Mr. Williams continued.

"Ah, Mr. Williams, this may or may not be true. Some found it easy!" Grace retorted.

After lengthy discussions, Grace was ready to leave because she was tired. Mr. Williams asked Akosua to wait in the reception. She immediately felt a little bit uncomfortable. She was also very tired. Some minutes later, Akosua heard a struggle in the nearby living room. It was Grace and Mr. Williams. She heard a bang and a slap on a face. It was Grace attacking Mr. Williams.

Grace suddenly ran to Akosua. They left the premises very much annoyed and worried. It was almost 4:00 in the evening, and they had to go home. Mr. Williams gave them 20 dollars to take a taxi as they left for home. They refused the offer. Akosua asked Grace about what had happened. She said the man had wanted to make love to her. "I punched him during a fight, so he ordered me off," Grace explained on their way.

Akosua got home as planned later in the day. Mr. Mensah's place was quiet. This was not usual at all in this house. She asked one of her half-brothers about where everyone was. She then learned that Mr. Mensah had taken his wives and the children off to a gospel church about three miles away for an evening service. Entering her room, she tried to sleep for a few hours before the household came home. The rest was good for Akosua because she was very tired. She knew it was going to take her some time before discussing her examinations with anyone in the house. That was even if anyone was interested at all. The thoughts of the day filled her. She thought of Essien and of the incident involving Grace and Mr. Williams. It was very hard to understand what had really happened. Maybe they should not have gone to Mr. Williams at all. She thought about home and her future, and then fell asleep.

Later, the deafening noise of the children coming to the house woke her from sleep. News was already in the household that Akosua had finished school. Mr. Mensah had gone upstairs. The old man was tired and had gone to bed. Mrs. Mensah entered Akosua's room. She stood by her bed and asked about the examinations. Akosua could not give any satisfactory reply. She got up from the bed because there was a special reason that had brought her mother to her room. She wanted Akosua to go to the kitchen and help prepare the soup for the day. Oh! Can you imagine? It was a turkey soup, a tiring meal to prepare.

After the dinner, she was told that Mr. Mensah's friend, Papa James the rich farmer, gave the turkey as a gift to her. It was to celebrate her completion of school. On hearing that, Akosua was so annoyed she wanted to vomit out all the food. She was also mad at her mother. After the meal, she washed the dishes, cleaned the kitchen, and threw the trash bag away. To keep herself busy, she scrubbed all the dirt on the kitchen walls. She decided not to worry about anyone. Her mother sat with her for a longer time than usual. As suspected, she wanted to talk Akosua into marriage; however Akosua brushed the subject aside any time it came up. Akosua went to bed very late that night with the hopes that no one in the household would ever bring up the subject of marriage again. As disturbed as she was, her intention was to keep herself busy and forget all the troubles at home, especially the trouble concerning the local rich farmer.

CHAPTER 2
Thoughts of the Future

There were rumors in Mr. Mensah's household and even in the immediate neighborhood about the proposed marriage for Akosua. She had heard from her half-sisters that the marriage proposal was on all lips and over the streets. This made Akosua very uncomfortable. They all laughed and teased her. The possibility of an arranged marriage to this old local farmer who was married scared Akosua. At almost 18 ½ years, and just out of the local school, she was a young person with a lot of ambition. Her father had initiated and supported this old, aggressive male chauvinist in seeking a new wife. Such an old man wanted to give a young lady like Akosua a sewing machine to stay at home and bear him children—a common thing in some of the rural and old traditional African societies.

"Not with me," Akosua thought. "These old men are really lost. The socio-economic fabric of the society is changing and we were no more in the sixties and the seventies. Women of today are trying to eliminate the social injustices in the community. My father, Mr. Mensah is part of the problem. The male dominance and arranged marriages in the rural areas must go."

Akosua was lucky that in the Akim Oda area and the parts of the southern part of Ghana, female genital mutilations were relatively unknown. It was not like the other African cultures in the country where women were subjected to greater physical abuses. Yet still the social injustice she had seen at home was just as bad.

The following Sunday, she knew her mother would ask her to go to the missionary house that morning and then to the church. They were to give thanks to the Lord that she had completed her

18

studies in the local high school. As usual, Akosua got up early and did her part of the house chores. She took a bath and ironed her clothes. She wanted the blessing of the Lord and a support for her personal aspirations, but not the type being planned by her family. She put on a beautiful and neat dress for the church. It was white and blue cotton linen. The two left for the church service that morning. It was not a time to show her to the public so she walked as fast as she could to follow her mother. She also expected Grace at the morning church service. They had discussed about meeting at the church briefly before.

Suddenly she heard a call, "Akosua!" She looked back and saw Essien. Time was not on her side because her mother was doubling her footsteps. She signaled to show him her mother's presence.

"Akosua," she heard the calls again. She pretended she did not hear him because her mother was an eavesdropper. She would report whatever she saw or heard about Akosua to the old man and the people at home. Akosua hated insults. It was not her pride! She was in no mood at that time for insults from Mr. Mensah.

They got to the church early. It was not surprising to see several of her mates and their relatives. They all wore beautiful clothes. Julie was neatly dressed; so were Ruth and two other girls in the same pew. Akosua's dress was in no comparison to theirs because some of these girls would do anything to dress in the most expensive outfits they could find. This would make them appear very neat, decent, and the talk of town. They would put on the most expensive clothing, even if it meant taking money from the older men they had been dating. Her dress was no comparison to theirs at all. The Reverend Minister was brief in his sermon. Mrs. Mensah offered twenty dollars as a tithing and thanksgiving.

Grace was nowhere to be found at the church. She did not show up and Akosua was worried. Akosua thought that Grace may be sick or something must have prevented her from coming to the church. She asked permission from her mother to visit Grace. Mrs. Mensah did not say anything, therefore. Akosua requested again. This time, Mrs. Mensah said yes, but she wanted her to return home early. Akosua went in a different direction to visit Grace, while her mother walked home.

"You should not be in town for long," Mrs. Mensah said. "Your father might need your services in the house."

The latter utterance made Akosua annoyed because there were many boys and girls in the house who could do the same work.

"My services are not special to anyone," Akosua said to herself.

As fast as she could walk, she left to find Grace. The two discussed the coming prom party and later went home.

That evening, Akosua went to bed early. In the days ahead, she was so mad at home that she even forgot to prepare for her prom party as she had discussed with Grace.

Although the final examinations were over, the prom party was not scheduled until several weeks after the official school closing date which was about a month away. This was due to a reschedule of events by the school authorities.

Akosua had informed Essien long before the prom party that he was not going to be her date. She wanted nobody. After all, she thought, Essien was no more. She wanted no one to come in her way to mess up her future. Akosua thought it was a good idea to stop the relationship. At that stage in her life, she was in no mood for any male companion. Secondly, she wanted to avoid any confrontation by her father, who had been entertaining the idea that Akosua marry the old farmer as soon as convenient.

The school compound was cleaned for the prom day. There were national and local flags all over the campus. Large banners welcomed parents.

Akosua could not dress up in new clothes as she had wanted for the prom party because she refused to accept the new clothes given to her by Papa James. Her parents, as such, did not support nor help her that much. Although she had been quarreling with them, they still gave her permission to attend the party as long as she did not stay very late. Akosua had borrowed a nice dress from Grace the day before and both attended the end of year party at the school.

At the prom, Akosua became very upset as the teachers announced the various colleges that had offered admission to some of the serious and good classmates. Their names were mentioned. Accompanied by their parents and relatives, the students who had been accepted by various colleges received a standing ovation. Akosua felt very jealous. There was one girl who had been admitted to the same school as her boyfriend. Akosua was very jealous but tried to hide it. She did her best to ignore them. There was an elderly man at the party who came with his young wife. He had found a new and younger wife besides those he already had. He was one of the polygamists in the town. Akosua did not even look at them. She was very mad.

She tried as best she could to make herself happy. They always had their funny little habits at school. As students these idiosyncrasies were part of them, and it made their lives full and meaningful. It was a good way to lift the spirits of a young woman who had great ambitions but was surrounded by very traditional and very negative parents who refuse to change with the times. At the prom party, the sons and daughters of the rich brought many cakes and soft drinks. It was simple merry-making. But as seniors in the school and the occasion being a graduation day, all the students enjoyed and made sure that the organization of the party was to their interest. Grace kept Akosua company all the time. They ate and ate as much food as they could.

Grace left rather early. It was almost nine at night. Akosua also had to get home before midnight. Although there was enough time for her to stay at the party, she also left for home. When she got home, the household was indoors. She went upstairs to report to her father and thanked him for allowing her out that night. The old man was awake and Akosua could tell from his face he was not happy. Akosua walked quickly to her bedroom to avoid any argument.

The following Saturday morning, Akosua cleaned the compound and scrubbed the main bathroom in the house. It was the day when all the households had to follow Mr. Mensah to his farm. It was an interesting weekly routine. She would have enjoyed working on the farm that day, but thought otherwise. She had to see Grace and was ready to come up with an excuse. After scrubbing the bathrooms, she saw the boys in the house ready to go to the farm. Suddenly, she heard, "Akosua! Akosua!" Her father was calling.

He then also shouted for her half-sisters. "Mary! Kate! You should clean the backyard of the house and the compound," he ordered them. "You, Akosua, you should go to the local store later today to get groceries and prepare supper for me before I return," Mr. Mensah added. "Now, the rest, let's move!"

He shouted at the household and they marched and played with each other while Mr. Mensah trailed behind slowly. Akosua watched them all go out of sight. The journey to the farm was like a parade of Mr. Mensah's children for the people in Akim Oda to see his household. Traditionally, it was a sign of his manhood in the society that he had so many children. Fingers were pointed at him and comments made, such as, "There goes Mr. Mensah's sons and daughters and grandchildren." This was what Mr. Mensah always wanted to hear. If this old man had such a pride in showing off his household, Akosua saw no reason why he did not take any responsibility in furthering the education of his children or encouraging them to learn a profession in any higher institution.

"What is wrong with this man?" Akosua asked herself. Akosua compared Mr. Mensah to the head of the Brookman household. That man worked very hard to send his children to good institutions. None of Mr. Mensah's eldest children was a lawyer, an engineer, a doctor, an architect, a teacher, or even a clerk. Most were unemployed or semi-employed. Steve always hung around the local cafeteria; John was a part-time bus stop cleaner, but most of the time unemployed. Titus was always at the Town Council area running errands for friends. Akosua could continue mentioning all their names and would not find one person to be proud of. She did not want to continue the names again. After all, Mr. Mensah's household was not the only large family in the town. A look at the McKays, the Johnsons, the Owusus, Clements, and others, indicated they were all doing well in the town. To stay in this house under these hardships would be tantamount to a punishment for Akosua. These were the very thoughts that had been occupying her mind.

With the man out of sight, what else could Akosua and others do but feel happy and be relieved of the tension in the house. She called the rest of the household. Joined by her half-sisters, Akosua cleaned and scrubbed the dirty walls in the big house. Time went very fast, and soon it was noon. The household would return by six o'clock in the evening.

Akosua still had some time to go the store and visit Grace. She got there in no time. Lucky young woman, Grace was still in her morning gown. When Akosua disclosed her itinerary to her, they planned to be together for a while and later do the groceries. For the two hours she was with Grace, all the thoughts and problems at home faded as if they never existed. It seemed her whole world now was with Grace. She was more than of sister to her.

They did talk a lot about themselves. Grace made Akosua aware that she had been facing similar problems in her household but not that as serious as Akosua. She had been advised by her parents to stay at home and help them on their farm. They did not want any discussion about Grace's plans for a higher education. The very thought of that idea made Akosua sympathize with Grace. It brought their relationship much closer and made it stronger.

Grace mentioned to Akosua about discussions she had had with her aunt called Rose who was coming home from Lagos in Nigeria. Grace planned to join her on the return journey to seek greener pastures and leave Ghana for good. Akosua listened very carefully with much interest and wished her the best of luck. She also expressed her interest in joining them whenever that opportunity arose, if Grace would only mention it to her Aunt when she arrived. The two later went to buy their groceries.

Akosua got home early and prepared dinner for her father. About 5:30, she saw the first boy from the farm with a very big head load of firewood, followed by others. "Yes, there they come," she said to herself, "the Mr. Mensah delegation."

The boys raced with each other toward home. The younger children and the girls followed but did not run or compete. The women then followed with their young children while Mr. Mensah stayed very late at the farm with his most loving wife for that particular day. He eventually came home ready for his dinner. Since Mr. Mensah knew that Akosua would not waste time with his dinner, he walked upstairs into his room and called her for the grocery receipt and the balance of the money used. Surprisingly, he had not asked Akosua about her examinations, let alone asked about her educational goals and aspirations for the future. She knew her father would never ask. It was not important to him. He would have wished that the old farmer man had come around much earlier and proposed marriage. That was the reason he had been spending much time with Papa James.

"Does he think he could get me to marry him?" Akosua asked herself. "Never in my life! I am a young woman of initiative and charisma, and the future depends on me. I could never support a man in an arranged marriage. In such a domestic life, I would be grounded as a subservient wife for the rest of my life."

With full knowledge about these developments, Akosua knew it was time for her to leave the household. She was determined to run away and avoid this marriage. She had seen other young women graduating from schools and colleges with degrees and becoming professionals, even with just a little support from their parents. Truly, at this time, she had her future educational plans as her top priority, not marriage or a boyfriend as were being pushed by her parents. She had been discussing this with Grace.

Everything looked so uncertain to her. She knew if she stayed in the town, she would be forced into marriage and given away to the old man against her wishes. This seemed very strange to her, but it was the old social and cultural way of life in the 1960's and part of the 1970's. However these arranged marriages had been changed in the modern times. Due to recent educational opportunities, some young women had come out of the bondage of old cultural beliefs. Many were working as career professionals in the cities. She wanted to be like them. However, Mr. Mensah refused to understand these changes in the society. He was not interested in Akosua's future educational plans. With desperation

24

and anger, Akosua could not control her temper at times. She realized then that she had to leave Ghana.

"But through whom, and by which route to where, or to do what?" she asked herself. If any opportunity had come her way, she would have left the home of Mr. Mensah immediately after her high school examinations. She knew, however, that this required careful planning. Akim Oda was her birthplace. Born in the post-independence young generation baby boom, she wanted to work hard and plan her own life. All that was required was a higher education. It was an adventure to see the world. After a possible education and a career, she could then find someone whom she would love. Thoughts on these issues engaged her mind every day, not the turkey and gifts from the old farmer. Akosua had no time and interest in that. She was serious about furthering her education.

Akosua went to bed at the end of the day and could not sleep well that night. She thought about some of the young women in the rural areas and social injustices they faced. The tradition of neglect, overwork, and gender discrimination was pervasive in the rural towns. She thought about Akim Oda, the village of Akim Awisa and other surrounding villages. She thought about the society, full of groups, clans, families, and individuals all competing for limited resources. She thought of how she had chosen to complete high school. Her future seemed so uncertain. Would she be enrolled in a college or vocational trade school? Akosua could not predict her future, but she was determined to make the best of her life ahead.

Waking up the following morning, Akosua was uplifted. She had thought in her dreams and vowed to find other means to continue her education. The society at home was not very different from any other African town many years after colonization. It was not that her ambitions were very high. The truth was that under the prevailing conditions, opportunities and social constraints, education was much more important than ever, otherwise a woman would continue to face cultural and social injustices. It was also much more important for the illiterate and half-educated women working 40 to 50 hours a week to support their families while some of their lazy men drank beer all day. Traditionally in the villages, the majority of the women with little or no education did much of the work to support the household and raise families. With very little or no respect from society, it was difficult for many women to choose professional careers and improve the quality of life for themselves and others. Some change was in progress, but it was very slow in the villages and remote settlements.

The change was easier for families with a good higher education. It was easier if the head of the household was educated and understood the importance of education. Higher education was the catalyst that propelled the change. Other families guided and supported their daughters in the schools and colleges in the country. Akosua felt jealous of some friends in the town. There were several opportunities for the youth in Ghana. There were reputable community colleges in the urban centers that offered various special courses for those who could not make it easily to the universities and professional schools. There were also many private colleges designed for high school graduates. No matter which way you viewed it, education was a priority program. However, the effort depended on your family and the individual herself or himself.

There was the premier university in the capital town; there was the great technical university and the educational center on the coast, not to mention the numerous historic missionary schools and colleges, most dating back to the early twentieth century. To make education meaningful, the government built many high schools. One was located in each local government area. These were the government educational trust schools and colleges. Akosua could see the nation was at least on a path to development. Education had even been compulsory at the primary level before. Students in various colleges and secondary schools usually inspired the youth in high schools.

During college commencements or vacations one could see the students in chartered buses singing. It was very easy to tell which particular school or college the group belonged by the slogans and fraternity abbreviations inscribed on the buses. Akosua could remember the very popular schools. On a bus chartered by students of St. Augustine's College, the inscription read

"AUGUSCO." The Adisadel College was "ADISCO." For Solomon College, it was "SOLOCO." "ABUSCO" stood for Abuakwa State College, and on and on.

Akosua wished to be among them. She could imagine the enthusiasm and the pride of these students. She wished she had enough parental support to have taken the College Examination earlier on, but she didn't. That was why she had to struggle to get through several years to complete her high school education. With the right kind of support, she could have entered college from high school at any grade level as long as she passed the college entrance examinations.

"Oh, Akosua," she said to herself, "there could have been a way out!" The truth was that it was not her fault. When she was in high school grade one, she approached her father to give her money to register for the examinations. Mr. Mensah refused and referred Akosua to her mother. Her mother also did not have the money. Mr. Mensah did not understand Akosua. It was a big problem. She knew her father had not had any school education himself. As such, Mr. Mensah understood nothing about what the government was doing to make education meaningful for the youth and all its citizens.

When she had approached Mr. Mensah to ask about the registration for the exams, Mr. Mensah shouted at her saying, "You up and coming girls are attracted by all this useless propaganda. You want to go to college! Akosua! Would you be going to school all your life and get married to your books?"

It was too much for Akosua. The old man just wanted her to get married, even at the earliest age. He saw nothing good in education. He believed a girl did not need all that education. There was nothing she could have done then. She was under his care. Akosua had to continue high school. She never understood her father. She took consolation, however, because out of his many children, she could not identify even one whom he had sponsored for college education. There was only Patrick who had left and forgotten about the old man. He was enrolled at the Accra Academy College with much financial and moral support from an

27

uncle and some other relatives. Mr. Mensah did not care that much about him.

Patrick was an older son, much older than Akosua. She had written several letters to Patrick at his school informing him of her plight. He replied to Akosua as a true brother, saying that if she wanted to continue her education, she should not look up to her father, but rather talk to other relatives, or at least look for a loan to support herself initially.

Just like the old man, her mother was uninterested in her higher education program. After several hours of woman to woman discussions, Akosua noticed that she was not even interested in taking her case up with the old man. Her mother was also scared of the man, and was thinking about how Akosua could get married to this old man in the village and settle to raise children so that she could have more grandchildren to play with. Akosua felt much pain and insults any time she thought about these events. After several discussions with other distant relatives, she realized there was no assistance coming from any place. She made a bold decision that was not the good news her parents wanted to hear. That was, she was not going to be a party to any arranged marriage proposals initiated by any relative. She would have preferred to have her future educational plans discussed.

Akosua thought the choice of marriage partner was a personal but mutual decision between parents and their sons and daughters. It should never be imposed or forced. The world was still wide open for her, and society was going through major technological, social, and economic transformations. The old order with negative beliefs that refused any changes was being left behind. She did not want to be a part of the latter. Her mind was made up. It seemed to her that Mr. Mensah's family did not really need her.

She was determined to find other sources to finance her college tuition, and would use any legal means necessary. The thought about competition in this world was high on her mind but she was very much open. After years of formal elementary and high school education, she could not just go waste away in someone's household. She had come of age and could see the changing society better than some of the old folks at home. There was too much gossip in the household that Papa James would marry her so that she could stay at home and have children.

"Who might have entertained such an idea?" she asked herself. "No doubt it would have been both Mr. and Mrs. Mensah!"

Akosua thought about her future. Her thoughts were filled with worries and her eyes with tears for the next fortnight. Her house chores were done with little enthusiasm. She became unhappy and a recluse in her own household. She knew that a change must come to her life. There was a need to hurry because her anger and impatience were growing day by day, and it was getting worse. She stayed at home for over four more weeks. She thought of Grace. All this time, she had not had the opportunity to discuss in detail what was happening to Grace and her somewhat problems at home.

Akosua thought of visiting Grace, the only one with whom she could discuss her future. She remembered Grace had mentioned a proposed trip. It was a journey to join Aunt Rose in Lagos City, Nigeria. It was the only way to escape the wrath of her home. She knew it was suicidal to run away from home, especially being a young girl. There was nothing else she could do, however. At any opportunity, she was prepared to leave the household for good.

There were several factors that were pushing her out of Ghana. The country had witnessed rapid development in the fifties under the white man's rule, until it attained its independence in 1957. Even then the country witnessed rapid development. Primary education was made compulsory immediately after the independence era, and infrastructure was improved. There was a rise in the manufacturing sector, which depended on imported raw materials. There was a decline in agriculture and a fall in the price of its mono crop, cocoa. Ghana, according to its first black leader, a great Pan-African, was the home of every African. Africans from as far away as South Africa came to live in Ghana. All Africans, even those who were not citizens of Ghana, had enjoyed scholarship grants to higher education. As the economy declined and the world political arena became complex in a changing social and economic world, political instability and oil prices set in, and the outward migration from Ghana began. Nigeria and Ghana were the noted countries in the West African region due to the pace of development, common use of English as the official language, and similar climates. As a remote cause, the country began experiencing hard times, scarcity of goods, breakdown in utilities and services all over, high cost of living, and slow economic growth. The country's economic problems and major transformation after years of military rule continued. Although endowed with natural resources, Ghana remained dependent on international finance. The domestic economy, being based on subsistence agriculture, had not improved. Heavy public sector wages, inflationary trends, and currency depreciation continued to plague the country. Luckily, none of this could stop the will of the people, because they were friendly and hardworking. Akosua thought that with continued education, and checks and balances in the system, the country could come out of its problems. However, she also believed that a number of the anachronistic ways of life should be done away with.

Akosua's own problems at home certainly were immediate causes that aroused her desire to leave Ghana. Her future education had been paralyzed. It was bleak and very uncertain. She had no career training and there was no possibility that her parents would encourage her to attend a vocational school. She hated the idea of marriage at that time, and certainly did not want to be forced into it. Her mind was made up.

She had planned to make use of the least opportunity that came her way. She imagined the consequences of her planned actions. She was prepared for anything. The more she saw her other colleagues and mates having their educations and futures planned with the help of their parents, the more she felt jealous and the greater her desire to move out no matter what the consequences. She believed for a parent to refuse higher educational opportunities to a child was unforgivable. This could have only happened in such an uneducated and polygamous home. She did not want to be a part of a home with such an absence of intellectual structure.

CHAPTER 3
Journey of Hope

About a month later, Grace invited Akosua to her house. Grace apologized for not keeping in touch with Akosua for some time. Upon arrival, Akosua noticed Grace was packing her clothing in a suitcase. "Grace, what is happening?" Akosua asked.

Grace replied, "Akosua, it is very unfortunate that the relationship with my family now is very serious. I could not inform you of what has happened in the past few weeks. My family is sending me to the farm in Achiase, a village after Awisa to start farming and later find a man to marry in the village. Truly, I want to get out of this town. I know they want me to join a man in this farm and I believe this other man—an old, rich, traditional man— plans to have children with me. I am sorry I have been unable to inform you of these latest pressures from my household. I am fed up in this house!"

"What are you saying, Grace?" Akosua asked.

"I have planned to travel with my Aunt Rose to Nigeria. My family does not know about this arrangement. As I had earlier mentioned to you, she came some weeks ago and is leaving soon. She lives in Lagos. We would travel by road."

This was a surprise to Akosua. She realized that Grace's problem was very serious. Akosua said to herself, "Education! Education! Going to school with difficulties. Oppression in the household, and disrespect and injustices for the young modern woman. It could not be in my generation!"

"Grace, I would like to join you," Akosua requested. "I will not let this old Mr. Mensah make me a fool in this modern society. Would you mind?"

"Oh, no! We can travel together. I have already informed my aunt; she said you can come along provided you are prepared," Grace replied.

Back at home, Akosua went straight to her mother and informed her that she wanted to leave the next morning to visit their cousin Mrs. Fati who lived about two miles way. Her mother hesitated but later agreed after consulting Mr. Mensah. Mrs. Fati was a direct cousin who lived in Awisa, a different town. She was always sending invitations to Akosua for a visit. Akosua's mother suggested that Akosua return by sunset the day after. Akosua packed her clothing that night. She did not take many items to avoid any suspicion at home. She had her belongings already with Grace. The following morning, Akosua said goodbye to her mother and promised to be back by evening the day after. Instead, she went straight to Grace's house.

Grace introduced Akosua to her Aunt Rose. They were on their way on the road to Lagos in no time. Aunt Rose had been in Lagos, the main city of Nigeria, for several years doing business, though they never knew what business it was. Grace told Akosua before that she might be in the catering and restaurant business. Aunt Rose had money and was in contact with Lagos socialites. Akosua had very good impressions about her. She was quite good looking, hardworking, forceful, and very liberal-minded. Akosua learned from Grace before their departure that Aunt Rose was schooled at the popular Akim Awisa Boarding School in Ghana. After school she worked for a year and entered a Technical Institute. With a diploma in Catering and Hotel Management, she went to Lagos soon after the government changes and when economic conditions became very bad at home. She settled at Ikeja in Lagos.

The three women finally arrived at the transport station in Accra, the capital city of Ghana and boarded another bus off to Lome, Togo. Togo is a French-speaking African country bordering Ghana. The highway from Lome to Lagos was very busy. After a three-hour journey, Akosua thought they would relax for a while but when they came to a rest stop in Lome they immediately changed to another bus heading to Lagos. There was heavy traffic on that road as well. There were traders and migrants moving from country to country. The reasons for the intensive activities at that time could be traced to the economies of the other West African countries in relation to the then-active oil producing country of Nigeria. The local economies in those years were not very strong compared to the economic boom in Nigeria. In those years there was much dependence on Nigeria, and migration to that country was at all time high. That was then.

At home, due to the massive education of the youth and the slow growth of the economy, graduates from the institutions had not found many professional jobs. The economy had not been able to absorb the high number of graduates in the country. As such, there were many unemployed and semi-skilled graduates daily on the streets. This also inspired a very high labor migration. The impact of the migration was both positive and negative. It had been so serious that in some instances it was impossible to find a member of a graduating class from the universities still in the country.

For Akosua, it was not these economic problems that made her travel. It was the social injustices and the negative aspects of the culture that did not provide adequate training and incentives to young women. The treatment of women in the towns and villages was more than one could imagine. It was a deterrent to young talented and ambitious women who wanted an identity and to be somebody with good education. They had class, and skills, and demanded respect. Akosua could not stand these problems at home. The lack of job opportunities and job openings for the women had been one of the reasons why some parents were not even interested in the education of their daughters.

Thus her father, Mr. Mensah had wanted to give her for marriage. She left and did not regret it. She was 18 ½ years old, black and beautiful. She followed her friend to Lagos, the sprawling oil rich city, for an adventure.

On their way, the bus developed a problem at Coutonou, a French-speaking city along the West African coast. A mechanic on the bus attended to it for over an hour. On the bus were a number of passengers, both black and white, including a white guy named

Paul, who was a returned Peace Corps volunteer from the United States. Paul had just completed his Peace Corps contract in Ghana where he had been assigned to a town near Akim Oda. When he finished his contract, he left for the U.S. but then came back to Ghana. Now he had taken on a volunteer job in Nigeria for an adventure. Traveling to Nigeria from Ghana by road was his personal adventure to see Africa.

Akosua talked to Paul for a while, and Paul gave his address to her to call on him later in Nigeria. It was already 7:00 at night. Grace, her aunt, and Akosua decided to rest on the bus as other passengers did. Grace talked to the mechanic who said everything was okay and that it was just a minor problem. The mechanic continued the repairs and was looking for the driver. The job was not done, and they could not even find the driver. They learned he had gone to town to find some food to eat, leaving his co-driver behind.

Akosua thought that the driver could have gone with his co-driver or even ordered food for himself and his workers. But there sat the co-driver looking pale and as hungry as ever. Grace's aunt immediately brought out a very big thermos and a food container. Yes, this woman was prepared. She dished out rice and gravy. Akosua ate with Grace. It was delicious. Aunt Rose also dished out a plate for the co-driver. She invited Paul to join them for the meal. Paul thanked them, but politely refused. With his experience in West Africa, Paul would not eat just anything.

Within a blink of an eye, the co-driver had finished everything and was licking his plate clean. These men on the roads hardly got time to find good food to eat. Paul and the other passengers on the bus could not help laughing.

It was almost midnight when they heard a whistle from a traffic police officer. He stood very close to the bus and asked the co-driver some questions. The passengers realized that the driver had parked the bus improperly. The policeman then came closer to the passengers and started checking their identity cards. He spoke to the co-driver in French, which Akosua did not understand. Surprisingly, Aunt Rose translated the language to English. Back home in Ghana, because the region was surrounded by French-

34

speaking nations, French was taught in schools, but it was only in theory. The students never spoke it orally except in class. It was a poor application of a good educational policy in Ghana.

The policeman then asked all passengers to go to a rest area close to the beach to rest or sleep. They could join the bus the following morning after it had been repaired. This was a good idea. Grace, Aunt Rose, and Akosua looked at each other. They and the other passengers on the bus left, walking slowly with their hand luggage, following each other. The rest area was not far. On arrival, they found there were several other stranded travelers in a spacious hall. Men, women, and children were all jammed together. There were about thirty people, including the passengers from the bus. This idea of providing chairs, beds and armrest for stranded travelers was noble. Although conditions were not very comfortable, at least a form of satisfaction was guaranteed.

Paul did not sleep but he read a book as others slept or waited. There were many police officers in the room. One of them approached Aunt Rose and suggested the women sleep in a separate room next to the main hall. Immediately, Akosua felt a little bit suspicious. She thought of it as an opportunity for the policemen to make passes at the women. She had heard and read about past incidents some years ago. It had been done to other travelers previously. However, with Grace and her aunt, Akosua felt confident that nothing of that sort would happen.

As they slept and relaxed, Akosua felt like using the bathroom. She got up and walked through the corridor toward the bathroom when a tall man in heavy clothing, but still displaying a badge, approached her as if he also wanted to use the bathroom. Akosua immediately turned back, but the man confronted her. He said he wanted to question her in a separate areas but Akosua refused and screamed. From nowhere came Paul. He was not asleep and had listened to all the noise in the corridor. Seeing the white guy, the man ran as fast as he could. Akosua thanked Paul and went to Hall. She immediately woke Aunt Rose and Grace. Akosua told them what had happened. They all got up and walked to the police duty officer to report the matter to him. Paul was already there and had told the duty officer what he had seen. The duty officer claimed it could have been a thief or one of the street boys from the town, or it could have been anybody. They went back to the rest area, but could not sleep again.

Akosua started thinking about her parents at Akim Oda. The adventure she had been praying for was now actually being experienced. She told herself that she must gather courage to face the unexpected. The ocean was just across the highway from the rest stop. There was a good land breeze caused by the differing temperature between the land and the Atlantic Ocean, creating a tropical coastal air temperature.

At sunrise, while some of the passengers took hot showers in the public rest area, Akosua, Grace and Paul walked to the beach to enjoy the scenery. Aunt Rose stayed behind talking to the policemen about the incident the previous night. The beautiful sun and lights in the morning in this French-speaking town impressed Akosua. From the rest stop she could see the sun way back as it emerged from the ocean. The sun was coming out from afar. The sea breeze was excellent and it provided a quite a beautiful climate. She saw all the beautiful hotels along the coast. There were mostly white tourists from France on the beach. Some were playing tennis; others were setting up their beach umbrellas, getting ready to sunbathe. The beautiful scenery made her think twice. She could see the government offices far away. Their location next to the hotels was to increase accessibility to the white business people and tourists at the hotels. It was not surprising to Akosua that there was hardly a black person around. These hotels were so expensive that they were above the income of the local people.

The passengers were soon called and told that the bus was ready. It had been put in good condition and was ready to go that afternoon. Grace and Akosua walked back, leaving Paul behind. Aunt Rose was already dressed and had on nice make-up. She looked very polished and was speaking to one police officer in English. Akosua eavesdropped and noticed the officer had given Aunt Rose some contact names on their route in case there were problems with other immigration officers. In this part of the world, traffic policemen and immigration officers took advantage of the high illiteracy rate and poverty among a large section of the

At the border in Lagos, Nigeria
Aunt Rose, Grace & Akosua

society. For the most part, they did anything they pleased. They took bribes and delayed motorists as they wanted. They went unpunished because corruption ran throughout the hierarchy. Aunt Rose was picking up contact names so they could have a safe and smooth journey. Over the years many anti-corruption messages by government institutions seemed to be changing the behavior of these immigration and police offices on the route, but still it was a problem.

They were almost ready to go when another police officer came by the bus. The driver told him the problem he had and then started a long conversation about other mechanical problems and how he had always struggled to repair them and had kept the bus moving in the long run. The officer gave the driver an address of a friend in a Lagos border post to contact. Soon the bus sped off and was seen traveling at almost 70 miles per hour. The vegetation all along the coast on the way to Lagos was interchanging but uniform. In some areas there were mangrove coastal forests or coastal swamps; in other areas there were coconut plantations, semi-forests, and others. Akosua could not find any major settlement. There were only the dispersed mud huts belonging to the many people fishing on the coast.

One other noticeable feature was the use of mopeds, scooters, bicycles, and tricycles sharing the same road with cars, heavy trucks, and buses. The bicycles and mopeds were very much in use in these French-speaking West African countries This was strange to Akosua. She realized that African countries were very diverse in many ways. She had to prepare herself and learn as they continued the journey. Except for the cities and major towns, the car ownership ratios were very low.

The driver stopped again upon hearing the siren of the traffic police. After a brief conversation with the officer, he continued the journey. The passengers assumed he was acquainted with those on the roads. About an hour into the drive, he parked the bus by the roadside again. The passengers feared and prayed that there was no major problem and that he could put the bus back on the road. It would have been awful for them to be stranded again on the highway under the scorching sun. About five minutes later, they were back on the road. The driver maintained a constant speed and within an hour they were at the border to Lagos, Nigeria

The passengers exclaimed with joy that the journey was coming to an end. At least they could finally see Lagos in the distance. Grace and Aunt Rose tried at times to catch glimpses at Akosua's reactions. Their eyes sometimes met. They noticed Akosua was never disturbed. She looked upbeat, very normal. Aunt Rose had had several experiences at this border some years ago. She was used to the hustle and bustle, the daily activities of the people.

Akosua imagined this was going to be the beginning of her new life in the great city of Lagos. Neither Aunt Rose, Grace, nor Akosua talked about anything they saw. There were just too many activities going on at the border and one had to keep a close watch on one's luggage. The borders could best be described as an informal market place and rest stop. There were restaurants, beer bars, photographers in their studios taking passport size pictures and loud music blazing from many kiosks. The place was not neat and trash was everywhere. Like a parent, Aunt Rose paid for everything on their way.

Paul waved goodbye to Akosua and then checked through the border. Aunt Rose and her party, however, entered a nearby restaurant. Looking through the window, they saw other travelers meandering a detour around the border. They were not using the formal border checkpoint. It was only then that Aunt Rose asked Grace and Akosua about their traveling documents. They had incomplete documents. Aunt Rose had not checked before they left Ghana because she thought Grace and Akosua were adults and that they would have known. She kept quiet for a while, then blamed herself for not asking for all the documents for Grace and Akosua before they left Ghana. They had no choice then but to find a way to avoid the checkpoint. The immigration officers at the check point were very strict and could demand very large sums of money even if you had incomplete documents.

As they waited, they saw many others far away trying to cross the border simultaneously. It was very interesting. With confidence they sat at the barbecue restaurant and had some meat and soft drinks. Soon after the meal, a man in his thirties entered and talked to Aunt Rose. Akosua saw her give an envelope to the man. He went out and came back about five minutes later with some other guys. The men collected their luggage while talking to Aunt Rose.

Just then Aunt Rose called, "Akosua."

"Yes, Aunt," she answered.

"Grace," she called again.

"Yes, Aunt," Grace also answered.

Grace and Akosua knew they had to follow the woman. Confidently they came down a big corridor and waited to cross the border. They went out to an open area to relax. They were surprised that Aunt Rose knew almost all the people around selling groceries. This informal, open-air market was bigger than Akosua had realized at first sight before the border crossing. It was crowded, noisy and very busy. It had been just one simple trick for Auntie Rose. Her public relations and social interaction had been excellent and was a part of her. It was also very easy for her to make friends anytime in new environments.

Akosua knew the reason, then, why Aunt Rose had been having her way around easily. She was bold and adventurous. However, she had had a few set backs and problems in her life, as she had not achieved much to her own satisfaction in the profession she learned at college. Akosua wondered whether this upset Aunt Rose at times.

While waiting, someone brought their entry passes to them. Aunt Rose gave an envelope to the gentleman, and they all left to cross the final gate of the border. They did not join or wait in the long line again. It saved them time from all the customs procedures and searches. Akosua thought the people doing this might be enriching themselves at the expense of the government. One could not count the number of people crossing to Lagos. It was in the hundreds and over. Akosua noticed that the border posts were merely rubber stamps or were an artificial border, indeed. She noticed some passengers alighted from buses and did not use the established checkpoints. They paid money depending on their goods and the possession of valid traveling documents. They had to pay more if they possessed no valid documents.

Akosua recollected that there were about four different detour paths one could use to cross the border. One just had to pay at each spot on the detour. It was nothing but bribery. She noticed, also, that there were guides who collected a fee and took the travelers through a bush path, a much more dangerous detour to Lagos. A third, somewhat unofficial border crossing was to board special vehicles heading directly to Lagos. Under this system, one paid a higher amount to the driver in charge of the particular bus. All paid-up passengers would then cross the border unchecked while relaxing on the buses. The drivers sometimes collected your traveling documents. This was usually an arrangement between drivers and the immigration and custom officials. On the average, Akosua noticed about a hundred people at a time moving into Lagos from all directions.

This border was also noted for crime. One could not even count the number of hawkers and other retail salespersons all over the area. You could also buy any form of currency in the world at the border. The American dollar reigned; however, some of the bills looked so dirty that Akosua did not want to touch them. They had passed from hand to hand, from underwears and pantyhose, and from pockets to a thousand and one pockets that one could not describe. There was also a black market currency at the border.

Aunt Rose had briefed them about all the scene at this border several times. Akosua had also learned a lot before from her schoolmates. She had also read from the newspapers. The bribery at the border was just part of the larger corruption that sprang up during the oil boom. The country had suddenly been transformed into an oil rich economy. This was a country where the oil wealth was seen as booty to be looted by few individuals who cared less about the national economy. Due to the fact that the oil wealth was poorly distributed, almost everyone who had no access to the booty engaged in bribery to enrich himself. It was not one's fault if he or she had to find a new path to the riches in Lagos.

"It would therefore not be my fault, as I was supposed to search for a new life to finance my future education. This is the place for me," Akosua murmured to herself.

Aunt Rose carefully described the links and economic activities that went on daily at the border between the adjacent countries. Akosua learned that first there had been an historical link between the people in the area. The border separated the black people of Nigeria from other blacks in the neighboring countries. She learned that historically the people on either side of the border were of the same clan lineage, but it was the pattern of colonization and wars that separated them — a separation demanded by the greed of the colonizers. While watching all these activities, thoughts of border separations of people of similar cultures were high on her mind. Each black person she saw resembled the other. Languages and forms of music were almost identical. However, the people were of different nationalities. She could not imagine a society divided by an artificial boundary such as these country borders. These were basically the same people with a common culture — a related culture though different in practice, but based on similar traditional beliefs and objectives. They were all black, brought up on the coastal lagoon fringes and the tropical forests. They were recognized by the primary occupation of fishing and hunting respectively. Akosua had also learned history at school in Ghana. She tried to relate what she had learned to what she saw and heard at the border. Now, this was the area demarcated by a political boundary into distinct countries. This was improper. Akosua kept on wondering. She thought the colonial governments that scrambled for the land in some ways did more harm to people than good.

Aunt Rose easily led them outside the corridors of the immigration post. They were given special attention until they left. At last they were on the Lagos side of the border. On this side Akosua was surprised to see the number of restaurants. International and local popular dishes were served. Fufu, traditional food on the West African coast, was served everywhere. In Ghana it was prepared with yam or cocoyam or plantain. The soft food was made into a ball and eaten with a bowl of soup.

Aunt Rose, Grace, and Akosua passed by one of the Fufu restaurants. Aunt Rose gave a message to the owner of the restaurant. Akosua could not describe the scene she saw. There were many citizens of Ghana here. Some were eating, others drinking.

"Hum," she said to herself, "most of these boys and girls look tired either from the time spent on their journey or from the work they have been doing."

"Akosua," Aunt Rose called, "you may have a seat." She offered Akosua a seat. Grace had already sat down. Aunt Rose, as usual, went on chatting with the woman selling the food. One woman was speaking the local Ghana language. No doubt these languages were also noted on routes along the coast. There were many people from Ghana and from almost all the English and French countries along the coast at this side of the border. Akosua estimated there were more than 20 boys and girls from Ghana at the border. It was not difficult to tell the level of education of these boys and girls had from their conversation. No doubt they were graduates from the universities and colleges. Some were traveling to jobs. There were others with no education at all. Other young girls, like Akosua, could not further their education at home. Opportunities in higher education were limited for the young women. The competition was so tough in education that you had to have the brains, support and the finances to continue in any higher institution.

Unfortunate ones like Akosua were left into the society educated all right, even if it meant only being able to read and write at the high school level, but they had no profession. They were mostly economically active young women without skills, vocations, or professions. Adventurous ones would travel to seek opportunities elsewhere, rather than stay in the villages and work to support the men. It was an exodus indeed!

Within a matter of minutes, they joined a taxi heading to downtown Lagos. It was not surprising that Aunt Rose acknowledged cheers here and there. The taxi driver slowed down because Aunt Rose was talking to a tall immigration officer. Akosua noticed how briskly the transportation business was carried on in Lagos. Passengers and bus conductors were equally active. The road from the border to Lagos was a first-class freeway. Akosua realized how money could efficiently transform a country and make accessibility so easy. The freeways were the tunnels and spines of the total landscape. The stretch of landscape between the border and the city was vast.

Akosua had much knowledge about Lagos from school. She remembered a lot about the big city. She knew it used to be an old commerce center and a slave-trading town. In the 17th century, some of the locals were captured by force and taken to the Americas to work for white men. Others were captured and taken to Brazil. Lagos was one of the major ports where the ships transported black people to the Americas. These were unfortunate historical times. She thought about slavery. The black people in the world had undergone too much pain in those years. There had been several theories on slavery. It had hurt the peoples of the African continent. On ethical grounds, slave labor was an insult to the human race. The philosophy and pride of the African personality had been dented and tainted. As they passed on their way to Lagos downtown, her thoughts on these stories became varied.

It was the first time Akosua had set foot on the soil of another large English-speaking country in Africa. She had also seen a lot of people from Lagos living in Ghana. Still, she was surprised to notice that she felt a form of guilt within her as she arrived in Lagos. It was due to the fact that Ghana's leader, a sociologist by profession, had enacted the Alien Compliance Order of the 1970's. It affected a lot of foreign nationals, especially the people from Lagos residing in Ghana. As a sociologist, the leader should have thought twice about the repercussions of the policy. The Alien Compliance Order deported mainly the people of Nigeria from Ghana. It was a very bad policy. Until the partitioning of the so-called "dark continent," the people were basically in one territory, separated only by ethnic groupings. Dialects of languages were similar in several aspects; cultural traditions among the Africans were identical. The partitioning created political divisions. The sense of belonging, of being one, diminished. A larger percentage of migrants, it was noted, knew little of residence permits and regulations of stay.

Akosua's thoughts centered on the fact that such ignorance prompted the enactment of the Alien Compliance Order in Ghana. It might have been necessary then in the country, upon assessment of its economic interests, and local support enforced compliance with the law. However, the manner in which it was carried out and historical linkages between the countries of Nigeria and Ghana made the policy very inappropriate and very bad.

"What will happen to me if the authorities in Nigeria enact a similar policy and drive all of us out back to Ghana?" Akosua asked herself.

She thought about this and foresaw possible repercussions if it happened one day. She prayed, however, that it would not happen during her temporary stay in Lagos. She felt very sad about this policy; she felt very guilty.

They got down at a bus stop in Lagos. Akosua noticed there was no standing still. Lagos, just like other African cities was fast-paced and beautiful. At that time Lagos, she understood, had about 6 million people in its metropolitan area. The city itself had about 1.5 million. Yes, it was her first time in a very big city. At least she knew that the federal capital was being moved to Abuja. She also knew that the population of Nigeria was large, about 120 million or more. However, it had been impossible to conduct a decent census for the past decades because of competing data on population densities between ethnic groups. Each attempt at a census resulted in tribal conflicts. The allocation of federal funds depended on the population distribution. The population was made up of major ethnic groups, each trying to outnumber the other. There were many other groups she did not know about.

Akosua did not have much problem adjusting. She wondered at first if the language would be difficult to learn; however, some accents were similar to that of Ghana. Activities were at a brisk pace. Open markets and traders occupied almost every available space. One could only count human heads. Grace gave her Aunt a helping hand in carrying luggage. Akosua helped with other luggage. They quickly followed a crowd crossing a busy intersection. They then boarded a local passenger bus that was idling in backed-up traffic. Aunt Rose made them aware that the buses did not stop for passengers in Lagos. You board and jump out as they tailgate or idle closer to a stop sign. Just as they reached the bus stop, one came in and they ran as fast as they could with their luggage and boarded the bus. They all gasped for breath on the bus. It was crowded. A bus that was supposed to carry 40 passengers had almost twice that number. It was a miracle how they even got on the bus. As the bus moved, a conductor squeezed himself between passengers collecting the bus fare. It was noisy on the bus with music at its highest volume. Akosua became a little agitated. The bus drove through a busy four-lane freeway. These roads had been built during the oil boom. The roads were wide and had pedestrian bridges all over them.

Two interesting issues Akosua noticed were that at intersections, no motorist obeyed the yield sign. Secondly, the overhead pedestrian bridges were not being used. The pedestrian bridges in the city were built to control the huge number of pedestrians who tried to cross to the freeway. Instead of using the bridges, the pedestrians stood by the freeway and looked in the direction of incoming vehicles traveling over 60 miles an hour. They would cross to the island if a small gap of time was available before the next vehicle passed by. The same was done with the vehicles coming from the opposite direction. The bus was now going further away from the city and later stopped a place called Anthony Station.

Akosua looked like a newcomer in a city. Everything was strange to her. Everything was new and everything moved swiftly around her. There was no time to ask questions or delay. Aunt Rose warned them to walk smartly and pay attention to no one, but to follow her steps and keep a close eye on their luggage, else it could be gone in a second. At Anthony Station, they boarded another bus. Akosua sat in the front of the vehicle with Aunt Rose. Aunt Rose greeted the driver in English and they started a conversation as if they knew each other. After a short while on the bus, Akosua noticed they were getting further and further out of town. Development was not intensive; they had approached the urban fringes of Lagos.

They got down at an unofficial bus stop, crossed the road, and entered a settlement that was more or less a cluster village. It was called Cresthill in Ikeja and was located at the northeastern area on the outskirts of Lagos. Aunt Rose led; Grace and Akosua followed. As they walked through the village, Akosua noticed that Aunt Rose was popular over here, too. Everyone they met greeted Aunt Rose. She looked bewildered. Children, men, and women welcomed them. Akosua wondered what could have made Aunt Rose so popular in the area. From Grace, Akosua learned that Aunt Rose had been living in the village for two years. Since it was a small area, community patterns were known and faces were very familiar to others in the community.

They entered an L-shaped block. It looked uncompleted. It was, however, in good structural condition. Since that area was on the urban fringes, there was much construction going on. Akosua noticed there were many other uncompleted or abandoned structures. Some were illegal structures. The local community tried to enforce their weak development controls, but this was very difficult due to the then newly found wealth in the oil economy and the resulting high rate of construction. As such, the local planning agencies had not kept up with growth in the greater Lagos suburbs.

In areas of the settlement where development planning lagged behind growth, property owners subdivided the lots themselves and sold them to developers. In such circumstances, it was extremely difficult to control development. A complete subdivision could be developed and built before work actually started on the drawing boards or before local planning agencies initiated a development review process. As a result, illegal structures sprung up on any available empty space, resulting in informal growth. Provision of services thus became a secondary matter, also dependent on the wealth and networking of the developer.

Akosua counted many uncompleted blocks in the area. In their L-shaped block, wood and cement blocks were packed in a corner. The place was very quiet. There were two other women in their late teens in the building. They were from a French-speaking country, Akosua noticed from their accents. They spoke little English; however, Aunt Rose spoke with them in French and a little English. Grace sat and called Akosua to sit by her. Aunt Rose introduced her party to the ladies. They exchanged greetings, smiled, and looked at each other. They were all in their late teens and there was some resemblance. Akosua guessed by the smiles on their faces that they were welcomed.

There were six rooms, a toilet, a bath, and a storage area. Aunt Rose invited Akosua and Grace to her room. Three rooms were used by Aunt Rose, and a room for each of the two ladies. The hosts prepared food for Aunt Rose, her niece, and friend. They all sat in the living room and talked that evening about the hustle and bustle in the city of Lagos. Akosua and Grace got the impression they were to look for work the next day. They realized that to pursue their dreams, they would have to work very hard and accept any job at all. Aunt Rose also advised them to work very hard at any job they got. They heard stories of other friends and relations who had made it big through the same kind of hustle. Akosua had no vocational training and was not sure of the type of work she wanted to do. However, she remained very bold and was prepared for the worst. Her training at home in Ghana had been under very strict and rigid discipline. She was not really used to this type of hustle.

On the other hand, Akosua thought her training at school had been more tailored towards a white collar job with the hope that she could have continued with higher education and qualified to work in an office. At this particular stage in her life, she knew nothing except how to read and write English and solve a little calculus. Songs like "Baa-Baa Black Sheep" and an unrelated syllabus on the sheep and the wool had been given to them at schools in Ghana. She was used to learning and memorizing to pass an examination, only to forget the information later — that was the type of educational system she experienced. She had also learned songs on winter and snow, even though she had never seen what snow looked like. Although she could communicate well, she realized there was something missing in her. Her lack of skills and experience in trade or vocational work hampered her ability to meet the challenges ahead. Akosua could not even type. Moreover as a woman, she wondered about the social injustices that prevailed in the villages of Africa and what would happen to her if she started looking for a job.

Grace and Akosua thought about the most interesting opportunities. Options open to them were either as house cleaners or in restaurants as full-time table servers, cleaners, or bartenders. They estimated and compared the options. There was the monetary factor about how much they could earn and save. Yes, Akosua thought very much about savings. She wanted to continue her education. Akosua and Grace then wrote down the priorities in their lives. It was Akosua's wish to work in the city for a year or two and then continue to college to study. The choice of the place for studies was very open. Her preference had always been to study in the United States. She planned to spend a year or two in Lagos where she could start with Community College, or to travel to America to go to college when she passed the required Scholastic Aptitude Test. She knew that with determination, perseverance, and dedication, her objectives could be achieved. She was not in a race with anyone.

That night, Akosua thought about Ghana. She wanted to know the story about the runaway girls from Ghana. She knew her father would never understand her. Akosua wanted no control from her parents. Poor parental guidance had made it impossible for her to achieve her ambitions at home. She wanted to rebel because she felt she could not be forced into marriage just for someone else's selfish ends.

"I will write to them when I start working," Akosua said to herself.

Her objectives were firmly laid out; she opted to work as a housemaid because she could earn a lot of money if she were lucky. As a live-in house maid, she would save about 100 to 300 dollars per month after all expenses. She had been advised it was better to work in a high-income expatriate home rather than that of a local businessman. She ruled out the option of working in a restaurant because the pay was very low and the work was very hard.

About two days later, Aunt Rose came home with a young man. He was to take Akosua to work for a Brazilian couple in one of the most exclusive neighborhoods of Victoria Island, a suburb of Lagos. Aunt Rose had arranged it without Akosua's knowledge. It was a big surprise to her. Aunt Rose knew the Brazilian family very well. Akosua was to be paid a 150 dollars per week as a live-in maid. The arrangement between Aunt Rose and Akosua was that a percentage of her salary would be paid to Aunt Rose for the first four months to show her gratitude and pay her back for the expenses she incurred on their trip from Ghana to Lagos. She had free food, a room to herself, and a job as a live-in maid 24 hours a day in the house. The pay amounted to 600 dollars a month.

Aunt Rose told her that the employers were very nice. Aunt Rose then made them aware that she was arranging a job for Grace in another neighborhood. Grace's work and salary were being finalized. Aunt Rose helped pack the few clothes Akosua had brought from Ghana and personally took her to her employers. Akosua was warmly welcomed. There was a cook in the house. She learned he was also from a French-speaking country; however, he spoke English fluently. Communication in the house was in English. Her employers had good English accents. She understood they had lived in Europe for a long time before they came to Lagos.

Akosua started working the following day. There was peace in the household and generally conditions were congenial for making a living. Her jobs in the house included babysitting and going on errands for the family. Apart from the newborn baby, there were three children aged three, five, and six. Work in the house was monotonous, but she was very serviceable to her employers. At times, she felt lonely as the days went by. It was very quiet and was worse during weekdays when they were all at work. On some weekends, she would look after the children when the parents were out of town. She sometimes took them out to the park to play or to the library. Akosua usually stayed within the compound of the house because there were not many errands to be run. Her employers were good to her.

On the weekends, a man would come to the house to do the laundry and some plumbing work. He worked for a cleaning agency. He also vacuumed the house and mowed the lawn. This man, John, was very hard working. Akosua had not talked to him since she started working except to say hello at times. She had been watching him closely. He looked like a good guy.

The mistress in the house also praised John all the time. Akosua felt a little uneasy about the relationship between the mistress and John. The mistress gave special services to him in the household when her husband was away. When the man was at home, she treated John very differently. One day, Akosua overhead the mistress describing the weekly itinerary of her husband to John. She was arranging a meeting with John somewhere in the city, but Akosua could not understand exactly what was going on. When the husband was not at home, John had access to almost every place in the house. It was very different when the man was at home. Akosua suspected immediately that something was going on between them.

Akosua later learned a lot about what had been happening. Both the husband and the wife were engaged in extramarital affairs. However, the husband did not know there was something going on between John and his wife until he came home unexpectedly one Saturday evening when he was supposed to be away. At that time, the mistress was out in town and did not come home until very late.

That night, Akosua put all the children to bed after reading bedtime stories to them. She laid down on a sofa in the room. There was no one in the house except herself and her employer. She wondered what was happening in the house. She felt sorry for him with the wife out of the house at that time of night. Just as she thought about this, there was a knock at her door. It was the man of the house. He walked to Akosua and they talked about the children. He sat by her. Akosua could read him. The next moment she was in his arms. He made love to her. Akosua did not resist, and for the first time submitted herself to a man, though it was mostly out of fear. She was very scared. It was quiet in the house; the children were fast asleep.

She could hear nothing but the nearby waves from the Atlantic Ocean. She could hear dogs barking and she did enjoy that day. She knew no sex education and feared she might even get pregnant. The man left and Akosua fell asleep. She did not know what happened in the house later. She did not know when the mistress came home. However, her relationship with the employer became a weekend affair and continued for at least several weeks whenever the woman and the children were not at home. She learned more about sex from this man. From that time on, the man gave Akosua money and other expensive items.

One Saturday, Grace called and visited Akosua. She had put on weight. She helped Akosua for some time ironing clothes. They then had lunch together. Grace wondered where Akosua had been buying all the expensive handbags and other personal items. Akosua did not disclose anything to Grace. Grace told Akosua she was now employed by a German family. She shared almost everything that had happened to her since they separated. Her employers, the German couple, had entrusted a lot of household responsibilities to her.

Akosua confessed being lonely and missing a lot of people dear to her. She did not actually tell her about her experience with her employer. Akosua knew Grace would laugh at her and spread the news to her aunt. She kept her lips tight. Their conversation later centered on their future. Grace said she would work hard for a year, save some money, and go on to continue her studies. She wanted to be a qualified trained nurse. Akosua had thought about her future, too. She had long cherished the ability of speaking several languages and longed to enter the medical profession. Thus, she wished to continue her education and become a medical practitioner or hold some other related medical occupation. Since she had run away from home, she owed it to herself to get a career in order to be very independent. In the absence of adequate parental care, she had to build her own future.

Akosua later saw Grace off at the gate. She had to rush for a bus. Akosua planned to pay a visit to her place when convenient. The old order in the house continued. It was the same routine work very interesting, but boring at times. Akosua was lucky, in a way;

the new baby did not cry that much at all. She had some peace in her daily work. The other children, however, wanted all the attention. There was some tension in the house. Akosua was dating her employer, and Akosua suspected her mistress was also having an affair. Her mistress called her one morning and gave her some old dresses to put on at home during her household duties. She was pleased with her services. At least the gifts were an expression of her appreciation. That afternoon, her boss called her and asked if she wanted to move to a separate room on the compound. Akosua readily accepted the offer because there would be more privacy. The room was furnished with a big-sized television. In the evening, she moved into her private detached unit after her household duties. Everything happened so fast and seemed so strange.

One day during the week her boss came home before the usual time. His wife was out of town on a business trip. The other children were at school. He called Akosua to his guest room. Akosua knew he wanted sex again. He told Akosua how beautiful she was and that he appreciated her services very much. The affair with him continued under the most secretive conditions. This went on for some time with no one suspecting. Her boss had been extremely nice to her. He continued giving Akosua expensive gifts and buying her nice clothes. Upon second thoughts about this affair, Akosua sometimes became very scared and nervous, especially when her mistress happened to be around. There were times when the woman would look Akosua straight in the eye as if she were sending her a message. This problem made her very unhappy, and she decided to move out immediately if any opportunity came her way.

As she laid on her bed one night in the new room, she had several thoughts. She looked up at the ceiling and asked herself several questions. Her mind immediately went back to Ghana. She thought of her parents. She thought of what might have happened to her mother. She however had no regrets and owed apologies to no one, but she felt she should at least tell them she was alive. Akosua finally wrote them a letter and remitted some money to her parents. Some weeks later she was surprised to receive a very encouraging letter from her mother some weeks later. She asked

Akosua to keep in touch very often and come back home. They were really happy about the money she remitted them. Akosua promised herself to send regular remittances to the folks back home and also to the foreign bank accounts she had opened in the United States and England. At least the foreign savings would be enough for her college education. Akosua felt satisfied with herself as the days and weeks went by. She kept the arrangements she had made with Aunt Rose. In fact, she had completed the payments to her, and continued to keep in touch as a sign of respect.

The Brazilian family who employed her had almost changed her lifestyle; however, there was a hidden tension under the peaceful and cordial relationship. She had good food and everything at her disposal in the house, but she was not happy due to the affair with her employer, even though the man gave her money and gifts. Apart from this problem, Akosua wanted more money to increase her savings. She thought this would enable her to buy a ticket to travel and pursue her college education. It was neither greed, nor lust, nor any extravagance; it was a reality of life. She compared herself to other girls who made about 300 dollars per week working in hotels. She thought she could become one of them.

CHAPTER 4
Akosua's Career

Akosua had been in the Brazilians' residence for over 10 months now. With hard work, much needed support and affection, she enjoyed living with them in the house, but she still thought of leaving and seeking employment in a hotel. She wanted the money desperately. She also grew more nervous and worried the more she saw the mistress of the house until one day when she finally talked to her boss about leaving the household. He was not surprised, but he did not know exactly what Akosua wanted to do. Akosua's mind was made up. No persuasion could have changed her mind. Akosua gave them three weeks notice to look for another maid. She had worked hard for them but could tell that the wife was unhappy. Akosua knew all the time that the woman suspected there was something going on between her and the husband, but there was no way to prove it. Her suspicions were not vague. Akosua could always tell by the eye contact. It was all over the mistress's face.

Unfortunately for Akosua, one windy evening, the wife was very annoyed and called her in. She openly confronted Akosua on having an affair with her husband. She was ready to hit Akosua, but the man stopped her. There was a very nasty moment with arguments between the man and his wife. Chairs flew all over the place. Akosua quickly gathered her belongings and packed her clothing and other items to leave the household. She picked up her suitcase and said goodbye to her employer. The man hurriedly arranged for a ride for Akosua to the bus stop from a next door neighbor. Not surprisingly, the woman was in no compromising mood; she was shocked and stared at Akosua as she left the house.

The man paid her outstanding salary and Akosua was dropped at the bus stop. The neighbor had been a witness to the marital troubles in the household. Akosua was surprised to learn how the woman came to know about the relationship. On her way to the bus stop, she was told that the woman had hired a private detective who had been following every move the husband made in the house. It was only the night before the confrontation that she got hold of the hard core evidence.

As if Akosua knew what was about to happen, she had already made her own arrangements with a girlfriend to move out to The Queens Hotel in the Lagos suburbs. Akosua did not inform Grace nor Aunt Rose about the scandal in the Brazilian household, but she knew Aunt Rose would definitely hear about it. Neither did she inform them about her relocation to the hotel. She was too shy to tell Aunt Rose. On her way to the bus stop, she wrote a short explanation to Aunt Rose and put it in the mail that very day.

She got down at the bus stop where her friend Theresa was waiting to escort her to the hotel. Theresa had been a good old friend that Akosua met during her stay with the Brazilian family. Theresa used to live about three blocks away in the same neighborhood. They arrived at the hotel, located on a four-acre lot surrounded by trees. It was really a hideout.

The bright signs of the hotel reflected above on the roof. It was a nice advertisement, written as "THE QUEENS." Akosua did not deserve to be a queen. The hotel was located adjacent to a newly developing locality in the southern section of the city. It was a low income, high density area built in 1970's. The hotel had 25, and all were occupied by beautiful ladies. The surroundings of the hotel were characterized by old, semi-detached buildings. Some of the old buildings were being demolished for new ones. Akosua had the opportunity to get a room because an occupant had left for another country after a year's stay. Residents paid 10 dollars per day as rent, exclusive of utilities and garbage collection. This seemed a matter of survival for Akosua. It implied that she had to work hard to earn more than 150 dollars per week to survive.

She had no regrets in these endeavors. Rather, she wondered how life at Queens was going to be. She formally met the other ladies, both black and white, already staying in the hotel. They were of different nationalities. She heard several different languages, from English to French to German to Swahili. Occupants at the hotel could form a small United Nations. Easy communication in English made them socialize. She noticed they were all after one thing, the money from the newly found oil riches flowing ostentatiously in the city. There was an understanding, peace, goodwill, and affection. Basically they were in a form of communal living, each with a treasured soul with which they thought they could help make their living and wishes come true.

Each room had a television, a small refrigerator, a toilet, and a bath. The rooms had been beautifully arranged so that privacy was most ensured. By all standards, the hotel was a place to relax. The furniture was antique, decent, and simple. What Akosua admired about the hotel was its neatness. The premises were always neat. At least it raised their standards. There was a security guard and a porter at the office. The porter worked as front desk manager and a clerk. Life at Queens was organized. Very few people except the management knew the sort of problems, hustle, and uncertainties the residents went through.

Customers, she understood, were of age groups ranging from 15 to 60 years and over. There was a big lounge and a bar adjacent to a swimming pool on the ground floor. The bar usually opened at 9:30 each night. Customers and patrons usually called on the girls after leaving the bar. Depending on a call, one could be lucky. The minimal fee was 20 dollars a call, if not more than 15 minutes in duration. This was a strenuous job, really; however Akosua thought of doing her best carefully to avoid any sort of infection and sickness. She was bent on doing this and earn some money to achieve her aim. It was such an environment that one could not go out easily in the daytime to avoid eyes on you. One must sleep during the daytime and relax the body. Akosua's room was next to Theresa's.

Upon her arrival, she had a terrible initiation in the first week. Being a newcomer, there was much attention on her. She was indeed forewarned by the senior residents. They suggested her intended services would be better provided if she consulted a medical doctor first. Initially, she did not take their advice seriously. She thought she was knowledgeable enough to control and take care of herself.

The seniors had earlier given Akosua an orientation into The Queens Club. The orientation day was wonderful. It was a pledge in an all girls group. No one was supposed to be on alcohol. It was strictly business. Akosua put on neat dresses. Her facial make up was done by a professional hired by the residents themselves. She also rehearsed the code of conduct of the girls at the hotel, and more especially of her living condition. The initiation ceremony involved a lecture to newcomers by the queen mother, the head of all women in Queens Hotel. It centered on maintenance of standards and contribution to a welfare club. There was also a ritual that concluded the orientation ceremony. Akosua recited the code of conduct and promised to respect others, acknowledged that she was not there to prostitute, but rather was there as a victim of a social and economic order. She promised to treat other people with respect and also to have a goal in her life. She finally promised not to make this a permanent job. Finally, she took an oath and signed the code of conduct. She was made to understand that she could easily lose her residency if any of the regulations were broken. At least there was order and enjoyment in the orientation ceremony.

A duty roster was prepared by the clerk at the hotel. There was a weekly rotation of work. The system was very helpful. It was all under the banner of keeping the environment to standards to benefit the residents. A duty leader had to ensure the maintenance of order on the premises. The clerk at Queens was a very strict person. His name was Quayson, and he made sure an inspection was carried on at least once a day. Inspections of the premises were such that one was not supposed to entertain visitors during those hours. Actually, the hotel premises were closed to visitors between the hours of six to ten in the morning. This regulation was made to let the residents rest in the mornings and also to have their quiet hours. The daily inspection was carried on each day immediately at these hours. Ladies with dirty rooms and untidy corridors were punished. In fact, what Quayson did was submit to the management director names of lazy occupants who failed to do their room and environment cleaning. They were very strict. An occupant could face a fine or an immediate ejection from her room.

Akosua had been at the hotel only four weeks, however it seemed longer. She had good companions and very good friends. Akosua witnessed an overwhelming rush on her because of her beauty. However, her friend Theresa gave her the secret in the trade. She made Akosua realize that about 50 percent of the men who come there must have some problem with their private life in one way or another. The trick was that Akosua did not have to have sex with all the men who came to her. She simply had to be very smart and perform oral sex and arouse them. Having sex was to be the last resort. If it was possible, she should avoid it, because after touching their most sensitive parts, most of the men would be satisfied and she could promise them a second chance after collecting their money.

Sometimes, Akosua regretted some of her actions because she was getting all sorts of customers. The information she gathered early on was that in such a business you could not distinguish between the rich and the poor, or you could not easily identify one who could pay the most. Since it was a money affair, one could not reject even the most ugly and shabby looking man because it might be he who could pay the most. She had been told earlier to collect her fees first and truly she was never found wanting in this. She was always ready to stretch her hands to receive. She had to use a fake identity to the clients due to the fact that she was afraid someone from Ghana might recognize her name. That would have been the end of Akosua in Ghana. She could never return if any clients from Ghana recognized her.

Her first customer on her first business day was a handsome, well-built, healthy-looking fellow called Thomas. Her second customer was a student who requested her to be his girlfriend. He wanted a relationship. Akosua did not bother to chat long with him because she had been warned about students by the seniors at the hotel. They claimed most of the students at the local universities did not have much money, unless the student was one of the sons of the rich oil businesspeople in Lagos. She could easily identify the rich students. In these developing countries, about 90 percent of university students used the public transport. The few who had cars were the sons and daughters of the rich. The poor students were only a headache and might bring problems, instead of giving comfort and happiness. A resident at the hotel could not pay the rent and support herself by following students. The third guy was George Lucas. She asked him to leave after collecting the little money he had. As smart as she was, Akosua did not have sex with these clients. She did all that she knew and collected her fee. Her third customer for the night was John, a boxer. He had good looks, but being the first time, she did not want to be very receptive. She just collected her money and went about the business as others.

The fourth customer that night was an old man. He was rich by his standards. He stayed a little bit longer and gave her 60 dollars. This guy was very interesting. His tongue was all over her body, and he wanted to enjoy his money to the fullest. She welcomed him to visit again because the old man did not really come for sex. It was the company and the excitement he had when Akosua touched him. On her first business night, she was paid 130 dollars in all. She was happy but was told the amount was a minimal income per night; some lucky occupants could get over 200 or 300 dollars per night. She felt extremely weak the first night but knew she would get used to the routine.

Her second day was much worse. She was getting dressed that evening when the director of the hotel himself knocked on her door. He sat down, and they had a lot to talk about. He said he just called to welcome Akosua to the hotel as part of his routine informative sessions with new residents. Akosua could not believe the director proposed to have sex with her. She refused him, though the man thought he had an advantage due to his position in the hotel. Akosua kissed and touched him as she had done to her other clients. Akosua could not collect any fee, but asked him to instruct his clerk that she was not paying rent for a week. He agreed to pay her rent for five days in exchange for the time he spent with her. He later left and promised to look after Akosua during her stay at the hotel. She knew then she could manipulate him. She promised herself not to allow the man again. That was his first and last. Other residents later told Akosua that was how he had welcomed each one of them. They had nothing against him except that he was not always ready to pay.

Just about five minutes after the director left, there was another knock at the door. It was her first customer, Thomas, the good looking guy who had come again. Akosua asked him to excuse her for some minutes because she had not had time to clean herself after the session with the director. As usual, Thomas paid and wanted to stay longer than necessary. Akosua told him he had to pay more if he chose to stay longer. He obliged and even wanted to know more about Akosua. He also asked about the possibility of having regular sessions with her. However, Akosua made him aware that this was strictly business and that she was not in the mood for any relationship, if that was what he wanted. He later left.

About thirty minutes later, George Lucas also called. Akosua told him nicely that she was not ready for him. She asked him to leave. Suddenly, the man got mad. He started shouting that Akosua had taken his money before and refused to have sex with him. The noise was unusual, therefore, security was called to drive him away. He swore to teach Akosua a lesson. He finally left. Later that evening, Akosua had several other clients. She made almost 280 dollars on the second night, and she was not having sex with all of them. She did, however, realize the business was very good, but at the same time dangerous. Some of the men became wild if she collected the money but refused to have sex with them. She got tired easily.

Her first client on the third day was named Banson, a businessman living in Lagos. Akosua kept very quiet as he bragged about the nice things he had. She listened and was very good to judge him. He was not smart but had money. Akosua could be even smarter than him because that was something he should not have mentioned to her about his business. She collected her money and he left when it was all over. Others came in and left. Sometimes it was very difficult to count and even distinguish the customers. However, it was very easy to count the money for the day.

Her next customer on the third day was an elderly man called Thompson. He was a pensioner from the railways. Akosua was surprised that this old man could be a patron at the hotel. She decided to give this old man a hectic time. They spent about 20 minutes negotiating and bargaining based on the time he wanted to spend with her. Her mind was made up to give him trouble. To Akosua's surprise, the man did not really come for sex but wanted to be massaged, caressed, and touched. He was so happy that he paid her 80 dollars for that time. Akosua took his number and asked him to call and come again as he pleased. Surprisingly, he gave Akosua an extra 20 dollars as he left.

Her other customer on this day was a university student. He was very different. As they talked, she got a call from one of the residents that the person who just entered her room was the son of one of the richest men in the town, and that he was good and very generous. Apparently, they had seen him walk to her room. He had good looks and was very presentable. He was Femmy. This person was so handsome that Akosua could not resist his invitation. He paid her and left upon agreeing on the next suitable date to enable him to come and pick her up to go to Akoka University campus.

Her other customer that day was a big-time lawyer, a Lagos socialite. He was called Tommy. He claimed he was from Ghana, and that even worsened his case. Realizing this, Akosua gave a false name and refused to even touch him. The man kissed her and paid her, anyway. Akosua had to avoid a situation whereby her name would be on the lips of anyone who came from Ghana. The traditional set up of her people at home forbade the job she was doing.

It was the same routine every day during the following weeks at The Queens, but she was saving at least 100 dollars a day after all expenses. Not bad, she thought. She had several customers of different nationalities from the West African Coast, from Europe, and a few from the Middle East. Others were from the southern African region. During the first month, business boomed for her. It surprised her, and more especially the older, senior residents. She got more in a day than she could have gotten in a week from the Brazilian family. Upon the advice from some of the senior residents, she planned her savings in such a way that she could send remittances home, buy enough clothes, pay for rent far in advance, and save towards her future travels and college tuition. She got in touch with Grace and Aunt Rose in the course of the months to inform them of her new job. Not surprisingly, they were very busy working in downtown Lagos. Aunt Rose referred to her scandal at the Brazilian residence. She said she laughed and laughed when she got the short note from her. She told Akosua that her former Brazilian employer had been looking for her in the city. Akosua called Aunt Rose regularly and also advised her pertaining to her health and the risks involved in this type of work, despite all the money. Upon her insistence, Akosua tried to visit a doctor once a month. Although she did not honor some of her doctor's appointments, her check ups were a priority.

It was a fine morning one weekend, and she had an appointment with Femmy, the rich student at Akoka University. He had promised to pick up Akosua to take her to their campus dance that day. Upon their arrival at the campus, she noticed that the place was very beautiful. The landscape was planned for an academic environment. However, the university campus's land area was limited, and the population density seemed high. It was a congested campus. Her thoughts went far back to the Ghana University campus she visited during her school days. She did not know why her friend Femmy was so popular. Almost every person they passed by on the campus seemed to exchange greetings with him. She realized Femmy felt proud to have her walking by him on the campus. They were yelling and shouting at Femmy all around. They were shouting and calling things such as, "One to one!" "Only you, baby!" "Wow!" "No hustle!" and "For your eyes only."

Her weekend with Femmy was unique because it was the first time she mixed freely with students of higher institutions in Nigeria. She heard very silly jokes from several students. She did not give her address to anyone on the advice of Femmy. He was jealous and afraid that Akosua would fall in love with someone else on the campus. His fear was based on the work Akosua had been doing at the hotel. Akosua requested Femmy on his last night at the campus to allow her to participate in the free-for-all dancing

Akosua outsmarts the guys

in the Residence Halls. Students, boys and girls, and some elders were all dancing in an open area to a local band. It was termed the "Lowering of Standards" dance. It was more of a rag and fraternity day celebration where the students brought out the worst behavior in them only for that occasion. She noticed heavy drinking among the students. However, she was moved by the music, so she got up to dance. Femmy stood up and followed her steps with his hands around her all the time. There were several female students dancing alone.

Later it was all over and Akosua felt good. She marked down that day as special. Femmy gave her 100 dollars on their way back to the hotel. She indeed realized that he was really the son of a rich Lagos socialite. Apart from the money, Femmy promised to pay her rent for the weekend. It was really small compared with what she would have made had she stayed at the hotel. This was because she could have made hundreds of dollars during the weekend. She did not care much, though, because she really enjoyed herself.

Back at the hotel, when she told some of the others about her weekend experience, they started hurling insults at her. They implied she was not serious and that it was not advisable to follow students to their hostels on weekends because they might all be coming to the hotel later on. Also, she could have been raped by other students in the hostel. They advised her it was better to go on a weekend with a businessman or someone who was rich.

"They were right," she said to herself. Femmy kept visiting Akosua; however, she refused all invitations to the university campus again. She made sure she restricted and controlled him whenever he was at the hotel.

It had been four months since she first came to the hotel. Akosua had been exchanging letters and telephone calls with Grace and Aunt Rose. She decided to visit them one day. She wrote a letter to Grace and discussed her future plans in the letter. Unexpectedly, about two weeks after she sent the letter, Grace and her Aunt called at the hotel. Aunt Rose was not very surprised at Akosua's savings. She said that if Akosua could take care of herself, she didn't care that much.

63

Life went on as usual until one day, when Akosua was returning from town, she was attacked by someone. Akosua recognized the face of George Lucas, the student who wanted his money back because Akosua did not go to bed with him. This Lucas threw a stone at her. It was in the night and Akosua fell down Lucas was about to hit her again but stopped upon hearing the sound of people coming to her rescue. Akosua was rushed to the hospital. She was hospitalized for three days. Grace called and visited her as often as she could. Akosua started to have second thoughts about the business she was engaged in. She realized how risky it was and how lucky she had been. She decided to change her style and the sort of people she wanted to meet. It was not the same each day. Akosua stopped meeting different men. Rather, she relied on the old pensioner, Mr. Thompson. This man called regularly. He loved Akosua not for anything but for fun and companionship. Akosua was in a strong relationship with this man for a long time until the man moved out of town.

Akosua then remembered Paul, the white Peace Corps member she had met during their journey to Lagos. When she had arrived at the border with Aunt Rose and Grace, Paul had left them to go to his posting some miles away from Lagos. He often came to Lagos, but only on weekends. Paul worked as a volunteer teacher in a village area. Akosua wrote to him on several occasions and he replied to all her letters. They continued to exchange letters for some time until Paul planned to come to a festival in Lagos and promised to visit Akosua. Akosua arranged a meeting with Paul at the local cultural festival. Paul mentioned that during the days he spent in Ghana, he thought he knew Akosua's parents. During a long discussion over lunch, Akosua joked and asked him about his experiences on the road and if he had passed through the informal bushes at the border before. He laughed and said no, however his camera had been stolen. He knew so much about the infamous border in Lagos.

Akosua discussed with him how she came to live at the hotel and the reasons behind it. Paul felt very sorry for Akosua for undertaking such ventures just to save for her future college tuition. Paul said she did not need to do that to achieve her future goals in life. Paul also told her about an incident at his village. It was a scene at the river in the village where he worked. Paul had gone to fetch water from the river when the local taps were not running. He was in the water when he noticed two crocodiles staring at him from a distance. He could not remember when he jumped to the banks of the river and could not describe the time and the speed with which he got home. He ran as a fast as he could. The two laughed about this for a time. The other incident while he was in the city was that he fell into a manhole which was not covered. He was a simple, nice person, except that his profuse smoking did not sit well with a lot of people. The two liked each other.

Akosua and Paul saw each other every weekend. He made her realize the implications and seriousness of falling in love with him. The issue of race never came up in their relationship. Akosua was no longer active at the hotel. They discussed a number of options and other jobs she could have done to earn lots of money without going out with all the dozens of men at the hotel. Upon Paul's advice, Akosua looked for a job in the city and at the same time decided to go to the Kings Community College in Lagos to learn word processing and to take a secretarial course. However, she still preferred to stay at the hotel and pay her rent as usual. That was the basic difference the two had. Paul cared for Akosua. She, on the other hand, realized that she was in love with him.

Suddenly, money became a secondary issue to her. It was very difficult for Akosua because although Paul's concerns were real, other jobs could not support her life, and her savings were going down despite her new job. Therefore, she sometimes dated other locals for the money. Paul knew this, but there was really nothing he could do to stop her. Akosua understood him, but with much worry and pain. She trusted him because he was the only man who had taken an interest in her, inquiring all the time about her education and her future life at the hotel. She had mentioned to Paul that she wanted to go to college and eventually study medicine in the U.S.

When they started going out, the other girls at the hotel had a lot of concern for Akosua because they felt the relationship was heading nowhere. A former Peace Corps worker had no stipend to pay for her rent and other bills. The residents were also jealous because of the other work she had taken and the school she was attending. Surprisingly, Akosua did not care in the least about their concerns until later. She had enough savings to continue for about three months. At that time, she wanted Paul so much that all other issues became secondary. Even going out with a white male never seemed to worry her.

Paul advised her to continue with the classes at a community college in Lagos and prepare for her TOEFL examinations. After that she could sit for the SAT before making any attempt to apply to a college in the U.S.A. With the local college education and Paul's help, Akosua prepared for her examinations at the college. Now, Akosua worked in the city as a secretary and was still in business at the hotel. Paul took Akosua out several times. Akosua paid her rent as usual, but rarely stayed long at the hotel any more. Paul helped her in all ways he thought necessary. Surprisingly, Akosua started visiting the library with him almost every weekend. He changed her character and had plans to take her from the hotel, if possible. Still, Paul could not stop her work there in its entirety.

The fact remained that Paul had her respect, just as he respected her. However, he was the only person whose concerns about Akosua were real. Akosua dated Paul for a while, yet Paul never attempted to go to bed with her. He constantly refused to answer any questions on it. It was only the last night before he left the country that he kissed Akosua, but it was only upon her insistence. Paul had to leave the country since his contract ended. He promised to keep in touch with her.

After Paul was gone, Akosua resumed her full-time activities at the hotel. Paul left a lot of household items for her, including a hi-fi, video sets, cameras, cassette tapes, and about 50 video tapes. Akosua displayed all of them in her room. She was the center of attention because the two big loud speakers Paul gave her. It was music all the way at the hotel, although she made sure she did not disturb others. Theresa and a few other girls always gathered in her room. They listened to good old school music from the eighties and the seventies.

Her friends did not want to leave her room because she was giving them good pop as well as soul music that they could not have purchased or listened to in any club in the city. Akosua had forgotten about Femmy and all the other close clients from those times. However, she started making enough money again and was prepared to do away with any young boy or old man who wanted to hang onto her for a longer time. She wanted no very serious friendship again, though this was very difficult, as she sometimes felt very lonely. Of course, she could have had a relationship with a nicer guy for a fortnight, provided he was rich. She thought of finding a poster to place on her wall that would have read "STRICTLY BUSINESS." It was lucrative at this time because men were coming to her at the hotel all the time. While in the business, she kept dreaming and thinking about Paul. She was still working in downtown, studying for her exams and also in her business at the hotel.

The director of The Queens suggested a video club be formed at the hotel using the films Paul left with Akosua. She was to be paid a commission when her videos and other equipment were used. Akosua requested changes on her contract at the hotel, to which the director agreed. She took a part time position at the hotel so that she could stop her affairs with men. Most of the films left by Paul were then being shown to the public at the hotel. In the city, the hotel became more popular as more and more customers were attracted to the videos and the bar. It was also cheaper to be at The Queens Hotel than most other clubs, at least in the city. Indirectly, some of the ladies experienced a high rate of patronage from different people from all parts of the city. Because of the success of the video club, Akosua struck a close relationship with the director. It was an experience.

She became more conscious of the surroundings of the hotel, the lawns, and the flowers that made the place beautiful. There was adequate landscaping on the lawns. With cooperation from the director, Akosua planted flowers, had the landscape replanted with new grass, and encouraged the residents to undertake regular voluntary cleaning of the premises. Due to their efforts, the compound became very neat and beautiful. The lawns were kept and the gardens had nice flowers. Almost everyone was doing good business and saving about 350 dollars a week.

Akosua had not heard from Paul since he left. Other ladies in the hotel teased her at times because Paul had not written to her. This had a big effect on her. She finally thought about finding a new boyfriend as a companion, a regular one who at times could be a source of inspiration and protection if possible, but not for any serious relationship. As she sat down at times to collect herself and think about her plans for the future, she panicked at the list of men she had entertained at the hotel. The list was endless. She remembered Thomas, George Lucas, John the boxer, Banson, Thompson, and Femmy, not even listing the others who came in for short periods and left. In all there had been over 100 in about 1 ½ years.

She wanted to stop all these entertainments and have a constant and permanent companion. Paul would have been a perfect one, but he was gone. There was really no one to confide in. She could not really count on or trust her hotel companions because the girls became jealous of each other quickly, especially because she was changing her life. At times she became confused, not knowing what to do. She wanted someone she could trust at all times, provided the love was there. Akosua checked her mail regularly, hoping to get a letter from Paul. She was taking care of her life. She was employed at the hotel; she had a permanent job as a secretary in the city and was studying at the Community College. She did not need all the men any more. She decided to take on a permanent boyfriend to while away the time.

His name was Lawal, and he worked as a chef in one of the other big international hotels in town, the Lords Restaurant. Lawal had been working there for the past six years. She got to know Lawal when a guy called Wizzy, a casual friend, took her to the Lords, a nightclub in Lagos. It was a memorable evening. It was there that Lawal approached her, saying he had seen her at The Queens on a particular occasion. Akosua denied it in shame, although Lawal mentioned names of her colleagues. She knew then that he was saying the truth; however, she had to deny his claim on purpose. Lawal asked to see her later knowing that she had company.

One of the reasons she dated Lawal was because he always had a free meal. Lawal was always giving her food at the Lords restaurant and Akosua had the opportunity to taste several dishes. Sometimes Lawal would deliver lunch to her at work. Other times, he would pay for Chinese food to be delivered to her at the hotel. He ran errands for her and picked up her prescription drugs when she needed them. Akosua really did not love him, though, because she knew he had been spending time with other women in the city. He used to boast to other men about the many women he had been dating. Akosua loved his food, services, and money. Lawal gave her rides when she was in need and later started buying her expensive clothing. Akosua began to wonder where Lawal was getting all the money. It was strange that Lawal was not even a regular at the hotel. He was too busy a man. Lawal, however, took Akosua to the nicest places in town. It was the same outing almost every weekend when he was off duty. They went to restaurants, concerts, and fashion shows. Surprisingly, he never asked about her and her life, nor anything about herself in particular. He was a man of instant gratification, born to enjoy life every minute. To him, the future could take care of itself.

Lawal was fond of Akosua. He was proud to have a beautiful girl like Akosua to walk with him in high places. Once when they visited the show grounds, Lawal discussed the possibility of buying out her video club at The Queens so he could start a new video club at the Lords. Akosua thought that was a very silly proposal. She refused to discuss it again any time he brought the matter up. Such a proposal would have been very insulting to the director at The Queens. Akosua brushed the issue aside since that would have been her end at The Queens hotel. As strong in spirits and determined as she was, no one, or more especially no selfish or self-seeking guy, would change her plans or arrangements at the hotel.

They went to a trade fair at the show grounds one day, and Lawal brought up the subject of the video club again. She told him off and asked him to talk about interesting stories. They walked around the show grounds watching displays of products from several companies from the USA, Europe and the Far East. Lawal was off duty that day. Lawal bought her presents at the show grounds, and they ate all kinds of appetizing dishes. The fair at the show grounds was an exhibition of local crafts and modern technological products from other countries. The function was a yearly affair, she gathered, with the aim of bringing manufacturers together to establish contacts, show products, and improve upon trade with other people of the world. There were several booths for the entertainment industry. There were live local and western bands. The booths for the breweries were especially full of visitors. Beer and other popular soft drinks were free. Akosua could not count the number of people in the beer hall. The concentration of people was like a high school football stadium at full capacity.

Lawal made her feel very happy on this day. One thing she did realize about Lawal was that he always wanted to impress her by giving her presents either in cash or in kind. He told her several times he was really in love with her, although Akosua knew he never wanted to introduce her to people due to her past life at the hotel. She had, on her part, failed to inform Lawal that their friendship was just temporary and for her convenience. Akosua asked him later that day to take her back to The Queens. In her mind, she thought that although he was nice, he had really overdone it. His compliments were very superfluous without any real love in them. At times, she stood up to him and challenged him on issues. She stopped following his wishes, as he always had his way around her. He never liked that idea, but there was nothing he could have done.

It had been more than a year and a half now at The Queens, and Akosua knew that all eyes had been on her during that time. She had almost every material thing in this world that a woman by her standards was supposed to have. Her savings were very high. However, her heart was bleeding. It seemed as if she were being haunted by a problem she never really knew.

The following day, there were questions from her mates regarding Lawal. Even Quayson, the clerk, and the director asked her about him. None ever said anything good about him. Akosua knew herself it was the end of her relationship with Lawal. Although most of the girls at The Queens had not been as lucky as she was, they were always concerned. Really, they believed she had some good qualities. She was well behaved, intelligent, and beautiful. A major fact, too, was that she was very polite and respectable. She was very nice to people. This distinguished her from the other ladies.

One morning at the hotel, Quayson knocked on Akosua's door. She was already up from bed and tidying her room. Quayson said hi and wondered where she had been all these days. As usual, he requested to be given something good she must have brought back from town. He wanted either a new cassette tape, biscuits, or even some food leftovers in her refrigerator. Akosua gave him some biscuits. He, in turn, gave her messages and some letters. She had replies to most of the letters she had written earlier to her parents at Ghana. Her parents had acknowledged other remittances and things she had sent them. There was also a letter from her friend, Paul.

"A good guy, really," she said to herself, "one who does not forget a loved one."

Akosua almost froze with joy when she opened the letter from Paul. He had sent his picture and that made her day. He had written from California inquiring about her plans, health, and everything at The Queens. In the letter, Paul remarked about the hospitality he had received in Africa and all the nice people he had met. He missed all the good people he left behind. He wrote about the orientation lectures he had been giving to the students in colleges about Africa. Paul raised an issue in his letter pertaining to Akosua's stay at the hotel and the possible negative impact it could have on her character. Although Akosua had stopped seeing Lawal, she did have a good job in the city; she worked part-time at the hotel, and was almost completing her studies at the Community College. She was doing very well by all standards. However, she realized Paul was concerned about the possible temptations of seeing men all the time. Akosua thought about it and vowed the best she could to stop the habit.

She was not desperate for money now because she was financially stable. She set a goal for herself to spend her time wisely on her two jobs and also on her studies. She became much more reclusive at the hotel. She limited the time she spent with other girls who had become very jealous of her because of her two jobs and her refusal to entertain men at the hotel again.

It was on a Tuesday that she got the letter from Paul. For four good days, she kept to herself. It was a big change in her life. She turned away all visitors, especially the men who knocked on her door. She did not receive patrons, but spent most time indoors. All her friends and the management thought she was not very happy. They kept asking her questions every day in an effort to find out what was wrong with her. Akosua approached the director of the hotel and discussed with him a possible change of room or a move from Queens She preferred a room further away from the other girls where she thought she would not be disturbed by men. She told the director that she wanted to be very serious in her studies. She had even contemplated the possibility of moving away from the hotel altogether; however, that would have meant the loss of the temporary part-time job she had at the hotel. Also, she would not have had the free rent she was enjoying at the hotel. The director agreed with her and changed her room to another level at the hotel. Akosua felt good about herself. She tried to be nice to the other girls at the hotel during the little free time she had

On the other hand, some of the girls had become cold toward her out of envy. It was safe to keep quiet at that time because she did not really know who her enemies were. Of course, she could not have ruled anyone out. The girls were all hustling, and jealousy prevailed among them as individuals, or groups, or where there was any social interaction. Akosua replied to Paul of the positive steps she had made in her life, and later talked to Paul on the phone. Paul encouraged her to keep her spirit and faith very strong and keep her hope and determination high. Paul also reminded Akosua to turn to the Lord and start praying, and if possible, to start going to church.

Akosua thought the time was appropriate for her to leave Lagos as soon as she completed her studies at the Community

College. She had not had any sufficient sleep since she got Paul's letter. She thought about Paul all the time, but failed to understand why Paul liked her but refrained from loving her. She asked herself several questions about this all the time, although Paul was gone. Her thought was that Paul must have been turned off by all the men she had entertained before. Akosua continued her work at Lagos and tried her best to achieve her goals in life until one day the unexpected happened.

CHAPTER 5
Akosua's Rewards and a Final Sojourn

On a bright Wednesday morning, Akosua heard other girls and residents at the hotel shouting. She heard noises and noticed everyone was running helter-skelter, jumping over tables and beds, screaming and yelling. "Why?" she inquired from the room next door.

"The police have called at The Queens to arrest all the girls," she was told. It was really a police raid on many brothels and prostitution houses in the city. She quickly put on her shoes and ran as fast as she could, but to no avail. The police were all over the building. The main gate and entrance were locked.

"All of us arrested?" she asked herself. The arrest was the most brutal scene Akosua had ever witnessed in her life. The police kicked the girls who resisted arrest. Just as Akosua was about to reach the stairs, she ran into two policemen. She told them she was a hotel employee, not a prostitute. The policemen did not listen. With force, they pushed Akosua. She became very disturbed and wild, thinking the policemen wanted to beat her. She struggled with them but was not that strong. Akosua got mad and with all the force she could gather, freed herself from the police and ran as fast she could towards a window. Thinking the level from the window was low, Akosua jumped. She fell from a second floor window. She was rushed to the hospital and was admitted. Luckily, her injuries were not that severe.

Her close relations, including Grace and Aunt Rose, heard about her case and visited her at the hospital. They were there most of the time. The other girls were taken to the police station. They were packed into a police truck which was very dirty and smelled bad. There was absolute darkness in the truck. It was locally called the Black Maria. They never understood why it was given that name. You could tell it had not been washed or cleaned for months. This was a truck used to convey prisoners. The girls were not prison inmates in the real sense; however, once they were arrested they were treated as prisoners.

It was noisy when they arrived at the police station. They were lined up and booked one by one. They numbered about 20. The police requested to see their resident permits, which allowed the girls to stay and work in the country. None of them had any work permit. The management at the hotel had informed the girls that everything was fine, and they were not to worry about permits. The hotel and the resident girls had taken advantage of the laxity of laws and the permissiveness in the society. The girls wondered why they were being arrested despite the fact that there were many other brothels in the area. Most of them did not even know the brothels were illegal in the city because they had had police and military personnel as clients, yet none of them had complained or questioned them. They were all surprised.

With all the oil wealth in the city, many of these resident hotels had sprung up all over the place. The inspector said he was waiting for the hotel director to arrest him also. The director, as he was fondly called at the hotel, came some minutes after. He waved at them and whispered that everything would be all right. He went straight to the office of the police commander. Surprisingly, they were all released on bail, but under several conditions. They were to obey the laws in the city and refrain from any indecent act. They were made to sign a statement to be on good behavior. They were informed about Akosua being admitted to the hospital. The director informed the police commander that one of his employees was admitted to the hospital because she tried to run away from the police brutalities. The commander promised an investigation into the matter. On their way back to the hotel, they all passed by the hospital to visit Akosua. They learned that her injuries were not serious. The doctor said she would be there for two weeks.

That night, the director called all the girls to the second floor conference room at the hotel and held a small meeting. The hotel was closed to customers that day. The director informed them that this was the usual arrest that had been going on for years. The hotel was late in paying patronage fee to the peace officers, which though illegal, was normally done to protect a business. He said these raids were common; it was the second in four years. His advice to them was to be calm. It was obvious that most of the residents were foreigners from the west coast. Most of them had no traveling documents, let alone residence permits. The director and Quayson left, and the girls continued the meeting themselves. They made many suggestions, one of which was that each resident should donate about 10 dollars every month. The donation would go to a welfare or charitable society in Lagos in the name of the hotel management. Over 300 dollars was later collected and given to the director, who in turn sent the donation to the Association of the Wives of Peace Officers. Most of the girls were very worried about the donation, or more specifically, the recipients, because their gesture could have backfired on them. However, the hotel management asked them not to worry. They prayed for Akosua's quick recovery. At this time most of them felt that Akosua technically was not one of them, however, they all shared sympathy for her. They sent her flowers.

The encounter with the police had given Akosua a lot of concern. Lest she forget, it was not her first encounter with the police. Sometime back, she had gone out with Paul before his departure. They went to watch a film, then danced the night away at a club. They forgot there was a curfew in the city and that they should have been carrying a curfew permit. They had none, and the police arrested them on their way back home. It was another experience she did not want to forget. The police released them that same night and gave them a warning after explanation. Akosua then feared very much for Paul because he was white.

Akosua was discharged from the hospital, and Aunt Rose and Grace accompanied her back to the hotel. There was a surprise party at the hotel on her return. She was still in pain and had been asked to follow up for several check-ups and therapy. It was an opportune time for Akosua to evaluate herself and her stay at the hotel. She really wanted to leave at the earliest time possible;

however, she had to fulfill some of her obligations first. She had a paper to write at the college and her exam dates were near. She also wanted to complete her contract jobs both at the hotel and in the city. Not surprisingly, two other ladies left for another hotel of their own accord. Others planned to make packing a gradual process.

"But where do they go?" Akosua asked herself. "Do they have to move to another hotel?" She thought that was unnecessary because it would have the same problem. The infrequent police raids would continue. Every brothel in the area would be harassed one after another. The truth was that although the local government had made prostitution itself illegal, not even a single local authority had made any conscious effort to enforce the law. Those who set the laws and others who enforced the laws were themselves customers at the hotels. The leaders and decision makers in the society were much more concerned with making money from the oil boom and had no time to waste on arresting prostitutes. Also, just as in other developing societies, laws were fine on paper; the implementation, however, left much to be desired. This was due to the fact that the social structure and the organization of local communities were that of a linked, extended family and networks of relationships. One would not be surprised to find that some local government authorities had invested in brothels and disguised them as hotels since it was a very lucrative venture. Implementation of laws, therefore, implied hurting and trampling upon interests and relations. Secondly, the growth in population had stretched and exceeded the number and capacity of police officers in the city. Most hotels and the girls residing in them took advantage of this.

The director pleaded with all the other girls to stay at The Queens hotel. Their presence in the hotel enhanced his business. Aunt Rose and Grace visited Akosua at the hotel while she was still recuperating from her wounds. Akosua, after discussions with Aunt Rose, formally approached the director of the hotel. They hold him they planned to hire a lawyer to sue both the hotel management and the police commander. Their case was that Akosua was an employee at the hotel and that she was beaten by the policemen. In the course of the struggle, she had hurt herself.

77

The director was surprised. After some thought, he pleaded with Akosua and Aunt Rose not to go on with the case. Rather, the hotel would help in Akosua's rehabilitation and pay her an undisclosed amount of money for the time she was absent from work and her studies. Part of the arrangement was to provide a specialist for Akosua to undergo several x-ray tests to find out if any internal damage had been done.

Akosua wrote to Paul in detail about the incident and her recuperation process. Paul replied and urged Akosua to leave the hotel immediately or stop that work all together. It was either that, go back to Ghana, or get into college. He really wanted her to find some other work. However, after discussions with Aunt Rose, Akosua realized she had much unfinished business before she could leave. She wrote in detail explaining her time, college, work, and hospital check-ups to Paul. She made Paul aware that she would definitely leave the hotel at the earliest possible time.

Akosua continued rehabilitation. She regularly visited a private clinic on Kenny Street. Upon each visit, the hotel provided a taxi to take her to and from the clinic. The doctor gave her some drugs and an injection and requested to see her again in four days. At times, she did not know what had happened to her, and she would experience severe pain.

She went back to the clinic four days later. This time she was made to stay longer for a thorough check-up. After several laboratory tests, the doctor called her and said her recovery might take longer than they thought. Akosua asked the doctor to put that in writing to the hotel management. The doctor referred Akosua to a specialist. The implication of the need for a specialist showed her rehabilitation was very serious and needed urgent attention. Fortunately, she got an appointment with the specialist the next day.

On the day of the appointment, she spent almost an hour at the clinic. There was a delay as the specialist had an urgent call to surgery. Akosua had another x-ray test and a physical. Other scan tests were also done. She returned to the hotel. As the taxi got closer to the hotel, she noticed a crowd and heard noises and the voices of Quayson, the director, and others laughing and joking at the front gate. As such, she did not even use the main entrance to The Queens. She used a side entrance to her room. There were no messages. She then locked the door, took some of the prescribed drugs, and went to bed. She was disturbed by knocks on the door several times, but she had earlier vowed not to open it to anyone that day. It was time to take stock of her activities at The Queens, or at least to have a sober reflection of herself. Appointments with the specialist were her main concern.

Not a week passed without a visit to the clinic. She went to the specialist again, this time for the results of other tests. This was very surprising because up to this time the specialist had not been able to determine the cause of the severe pains she had been having, nor whether she had broken any bones during her fall. During this time Akosua was paid by the hotel for her part-time job although she was on an extended leave of absence. She was also lucky to be given a paid leave of absence from her other job in the city. However, she had a very short time to prepare for her SAT examinations at the Community College. Thus, she had to spend her time between healing, learning, and putting her life back together. Her visits to the specialist were almost done as the pains took time to heal. She was getting better and better. Support from Aunt Rose, Grace, and Paul made her recover very quickly.

Akosua resumed her part-time work at the hotel, and later fully resumed her part-time work in the city. On her return to a full and normal life, everybody welcomed her with open arms and gifts. She spent most of her time in between jobs preparing for the SAT examinations. The day she took the exam was unlike any other examination day. She was prepared and had matured in her thoughts. She came back from the examination hall expecting high scores.

During all this time, Akosua was thinking about leaving Lagos. She had been discussing with Paul the possibility of admission to a college in the United States. Paul was prepared to help her. Not surprisingly, he was happy for Akosua and sent her an invitation letter. He had earlier prompted her to apply to a college in the county where he was living in the United States. Paul had made it very clear to Akosua that he was eager to help her achieve her dream. He was not interested in love or marital affairs; however, Akosua wanted him more than that. She really thought as time went by that Paul would change his mind. Paul took his time to write and explain to Akosua the immigration issues in the United States. He asked Akosua to visit the U.S. Information and Cultural Centers to read more about the immigration issues.

Akosua knew she had to leave. She had spent time packing and making arrangements to leave the city altogether. The police action at the hotel had compounded her personal problems. She did not spend any of her savings in Lagos for any unnecessary items. She made sure to economize on what items she did buy. Her total savings was over 6,000 dollars. This did not include the payment made by the hotel for the assault and casualty suffered during the police raid. It also excluded the value of all her personal items and those the hotel was still using at the video club.

Now, most of the residents at The Queens could tell Akosua was a different person who had put her life back together. Some weeks later, Quayson called her, "Akosua, Akosua!"

"Come in, Quayson," she replied. As usual, he brought her several letters and messages. There were notes from Lawal, Wizzy, and a host of greetings from several unrecognized people who must have heard of her tragedy lately. They were all wishing her the best of luck and a speedy recovery. Their letters had come late, though she appreciated the thought.

"Are you still afraid of the police?" Quayson asked. "You look very worried," he continued.

"Yes, and I am still considering whether I should continue to stay at this place or not," Akosua replied.

Quayson thought it was the police harassment that had made her worried, or that she was sick. Quayson, not knowing about her plans, went back to the office and informed the director. The director called Akosua to his office to be sure she had no more problems. He advised Akosua to put all fears away and that the police would not come to the hotel again.

There was one letter that Akosua had forgotten to open. It was the results from the SAT examinations. Akosua exclaimed with joy upon reading the results. She had very high SAT scores.

She told herself that this was the time to leave and travel to America to meet Paul. She forwarded the results to Paul, who sent them with her admission package to the college she had chosen. With Paul's assistance, the admission procedures to a college in the United States were finalized.

Back at the hotel, Akosua started preparations to leave. She informed the director upon the instructions of Paul and terminated the working contracts she had with the hotel. Actually, her plan was to go back to Ghana, leave all her things to the family of Mr. Mensah, and then travel to America to study. Her goal was to become a doctor or settle for a profession in the health sector. She made telephone calls to some friends she knew in London to send her invitation letters so she could visit them in transit. In fact, she talked to Paul more often. Finally, the date of her departure from the hotel was very near. The director, after accepting her request to leave, wanted to plan a party for her, which she refused. The director was really hurt by Akosua's departure, although she could not say the same was true of the other girls.

On the date of her departure, she signed off from the hotel residence. The director and Quayson came to see her off. Aunt Rose, Grace, Theresa, her close relatives and a few friends came to see her off, as well. Akosua rented a truck which ran a moving service between Nigeria and Ghana The truck came to The Queens and loaded all her items. She said goodbye to all her friends in Lagos and left with joy and pain at the same time. Her departure suddenly turned into something she did not expect. There were a few girls and friends in the area almost in tears. She was sad but was happy to leave with much excitement. She felt that her adventure in Lagos was over. The journey back to Ghana was not as tedious as she had experienced some years ago.

Back at home in Ghana, Akosua was given a huge reception by her parents. They were very receptive. Her people and family accepted her with wide open arms. Due to the frequent remittances she made to them, Mr. and Mrs. Mensah were very happy to see her return with all the material possessions. She carried about ten suitcases of clothing, not counting the boxes of shoes, television sets, radios and other items. Her folks at home were very materialistic. Since she brought a lot of items and clothing to them, her mother was in the best mood of all. Apart from that, Akosua had matured, and her mother talked to her politely. They had forgotten that she ran away from home. Her father was especially impressed, first by the number of gifts given to him, and then by the amount of money she gave to the family. There was a big party for her at home, although Akosua had to finance everything. She still knew she had a future.

Akosua spent a month at home, then bought a ticket and left the country. Her expectations of meeting Paul again and starting a whole new life were high. She left for the United States after a brief stop in London. Upon her arrival in the United States, Akosua first stayed with an old family friend in the mountain states. It was in the month of December. The winter was very severe. On her day of arrival, the area had just had a serious snowstorm—about seventeen inches of snow fell. Can you imagine! It was the first time she shad seen snow, although she had learned about it in Ghana almost 20 years ago. She had been made to memorize songs about snow, but did not see snow until she was almost twenty years old! Akosua still knew how to sing the old songs about snow. She was curious, but not that amazed.

Her arrival in the mountain states was just a stop over. There was an old family friend of Mr. Mensah who had been living in the United States for many years. This friend had learned about Akosua's sudden departure from Ghana when he visited one holiday. Akosua started communicating with him through her mother. Her itinerary was to stay with this family friend for a few days before moving to join Paul in Los Angeles. During her flight to the mountain states, Akosua also experienced one of the most turbulent storms in flight. Above 40,000 feet, the airplane started rattling in mid-air, and she was almost tossed from her seat. Her stomach started trembling, and her body was shaken. She was scared on this flight.

After a week in the mountain states, Akosua joined Paul in Los Angeles. Paul welcomed Akosua with some friends at the airport. She was very happy to see Paul again. He had grown a beard and had put on much weight since he left Africa. Paul allowed Akosua to stay with him for some time. Although they were not romantically involved, they lived together and did everything as lovers, except make love. It was not very surprising to her that Paul had no interest in women. It was not only Akosua, but he was really not interested in women altogether. He never dated anyone and had no girlfriend. Akosua became a little bit suspicious of him and was afraid he might be dating men. She was not against him being gay, assuming he was. However, Akosua had not been exposed to that kind of life.

During her first weeks in the States, Paul accompanied Akosua to the campus where she was to enroll. On their way, Paul introduced Akosua to an old friend, a woman, and Akosua shook hands with her. Akosua shook her hand by scratching her palm like she had done back in Africa. Surprisingly, the woman later told Paul that Akosua might be a lesbian because she thought Akosua might have been making a pass at her. Akosua did not even know what a lesbian looked like. It made her feel very bad. Paul took time to explain to Akosua about the controversial issues on the sexes especially gays and lesbians in the United States. Akosua contacted the lady just to prove to her that she was trying to be nice. The greeting was the cordial gesture she used to do in Africa with her friends. Later, they became very good friends.

When this issue came up, Akosua wanted Paul to prove that he was not one of them; she tried the best she could to go to bed with him, but Paul refused. Truly, they slept in separate bedrooms. Paul had really changed. He finally made it very clear to Akosua that he did not mind helping her get settled, however, he was not interested in romance at all and that she forget any wishes of romantic involvement with him. Akosua took his word, and they became the best of friends.

During those few weeks after her arrival, another incident happened at their apartment that made Akosua feel nervous any time she walked through the streets in the neighborhood. One day when Paul had already gone to school, Akosua washed one of her nice dresses and went out to the rooftop to hang the dress to dry in the sun. Unfortunately, there was bang, and the door to the roof top closed with the force of the wind. The door to their apartment was not closed, and she had even left the iron on. Leaning over the wall, she tried to get some attention from people on the street seven stories below. Akosua heard shouts from some elderly women, pleading with her not to jump. She was scared and did not know what was going on. She became more and more confused, when suddenly, the ambulance service from the rescue squad arrived. Some talked to her from below while others came up to rescue her. It was very strange. Akosua did not know the elderly women had telephoned the police and told them someone was about to commit suicide by jumping off the roof. When she explained herself to the rescue team, they laughed, understood, and let her go. She was so embarrassed that for three days she refused to go into the streets. Residents laughed at her anytime she walked down the street. Paul also laughed, but sympathized with her when he came home that night.

About six weeks after her arrival, and after finalizing her enrollment at the community college, Akosua applied for a permit to work part-time. She worked as a maid in one of the suburbs. Her employers were Jewish and had migrated from South Africa. They were very strict with her. She had to conform to their wishes and work according to the schedule prepared for her. She was paid 200 dollars a week, but this did not include room and board. The work usually involved picking up the couple's son from school, which was within walking distance, at 2:00 each afternoon, then caring for the boy until his parents returned from work.

Her work schedule was from 2:00 p.m. to 7:00 p.m. each day, except for weekends. It reminded her of the experience with the Brazilian couple back in Nigeria. However, Akosua had learned that lesson and swore never to repeat it.

Although she was with Paul, she found life in the United States very strange. People were too busy and very individualistic. There was very little togetherness; it seemed as if each person had to care for him or herself. This issue was initially irrelevant and of no concern to her; however, as time went by, she felt very lonely, except the few times she and Paul went out to dinner and attended functions together. Paul himself was very busy. He was trying to complete his graduate program and holding two part-time jobs at

84

the same time one in the library on his campus, and also as a pizza delivery person. Paul had very little time to socialize and he studied at least free time he could get. Thus it made Akosua also very serious about her studies. Every morning at 7:00, she got up and took the bus to the college campus. Her lectures started at half past eight and lasted till mid-day. She then went to her job with the Jewish family.

The college had almost 5,000 students, including the non-resident student population. Akosua was surprised by a number of organizations, clubs, with their different issues and agendas on campus. African American students had a society that was very different from the African students' society. There were so many societies based on ethnicity and race that Akosua did not understand them all. She had expected the student population to belong to one big Student Union. She felt very lonely on campus but tried to adjust. She tried to be friendly with several groups of black females but always got strange feelings and looks from them. No one was prepared to spend enough time with her.

It seemed everyone was either busy doing his or her homework or leaving to go to work. It became very obvious to her that this society was driven by the economic trends of the day. Almost everyone she saw or met was busy working very hard to make ends meet. It took her a long time to read and understand American history. She realized that blacks in the society had been shaped by the American culture — they were not African at all. The few Africans she met had also forgotten where they had come from and had adopted the American way of life. The rapid technological advancement of the Americas and the distant separation from the African continent had a major impact on the people of African descent.

It took her a long time to understand that there were basic cultural differences between the Africans in Africa, the Africans in the United States, and the African-Americans. It took her even longer to realize that life in the United States was different than life in Europe, and even more different than the lesser-developed countries in Africa. Coming from Africa, she had been shaped by that culture in her dressing and eating habits, in her language and communication, in her attitude to life in general. At first, she blamed everyone around her. She blamed them because they were not interested in her and her affairs. She blamed people any time they told her they were too busy to listen to her. It took her some time before she adjusted to the American way of life.

Akosua's whole life changed for the better during her college days as she began to understand what life was all about, and learned the right from wrong in this society. The tough experiences she'd had made her a very serious student. During her four years at college, she was totally transformed. She realized she was becoming more of an American. Her dressing changed; her food tastes changed; so did her communication and language. She loved the American way of life but had to work all the time and had little time to spend with people. She worked two part-time jobs with all the seriousness she could muster, just to pay her bills. Although she was attending an inter-denominational Christian church, it was not on a regular basis. She felt sorry for herself when she looked back. She finally realized that people are shaped by the society they live in. There was no need to blame people now. She understood where people came from and also understood their actions. She became much like a black living the American dream when she graduated with a degree in Biostatistics after four years of college. She forgave her parents for their neglect and the troubles she had gone through. They lived in an old world.

Although things have changed, it is Akosua's wish that parents give their daughters the best they can to make their education a top priority. She realizes the path she took to make the American dream a reality was not the best; however, she would not want any girl to experience the worst, as she did in Lagos, Nigeria. Her advice to parents all over the world is that they should give the best to their teenage girls and guide them to prevent them from abuse. Parents should sacrifice and provide for their daughters. Akosua has learned from her experience. Now that she *is* somebody, the story about her past is being told so that others can learn from her mistakes.

This book has focused on some of the problems facing young women in developing countries especially in some parts of Africa. These problems have included neglect, abuse and overwork. It has highlighted some of the images of female upbringing as shaped and affected by conflicts between culture and female development. Although progress is being made in many places to promote gender equity in education and eliminate economic disparities between genders, there is still work to be done.

I have known Akosua through her years in Ghana and her struggles in Lagos, Nigeria and also in the U.S. Akosua was able to overcome her trials and risky adventures in life and became a successful medical bio-statistician. My objective in writing this book is to come out with some hard truth about the struggles of other unfortunate young women in the cities of Africa, who have resorted to prostitution as way out of the prevailing economic hardship. It is my belief that given the right opportunities, many of these young women will triumph over their adversities.

Akosua's experience also shows that no matter how far one falls and experiences problems in life, there is real life at the end of every tunnel.